Stephen Crane's
THE RED BADGE
OF
COURAGE

NOTES

Edited and with an Introduction by
HAROLD BLOOM

© 1996 by Chelsea House Publishers, a division of Main Line Book Co.

Introduction © 1996 by Harold Bloom

Printed and bound in the United States of America.

First Printing
1 3 5 7 9 8 6 4 2

ISBN: 0-7910-3695-2

Chelsea House Publishers
1974 Sproul Road, Suite 400
P.O. Box 914
Broomall, PA 19008-0914

Contents

User's Guide

This volume is designed to present biographical, critical, and bibliographical information on Stephen Crane and *The Red Badge of Courage*. Following Harold Bloom's introduction, there appears a detailed biography of the author, discussing the major events in his life and his important literary works. Then follows a thematic and structural analysis of the work, in which significant themes, patterns, and motifs are traced. An annotated list of characters supplies brief information on the chief characters in the work.

A selection of critical extracts, derived from previously published material by leading critics, then follows. The extracts consist of statements by the author on his work, early reviews of the work, and later evaluations down to the present day. The items are arranged chronologically by date of first publication. A bibliography of Crane's writings (including a complete listing of all books he wrote, cowrote, edited, and translated in his lifetime, and important posthumous publications), a list of additional books and articles on him and on *The Red Badge of Courage,* and an index of themes and ideas conclude the volume.

Harold Bloom is Sterling Professor of the Humanities at Yale University and Henry W. and Albert A. Berg Professor of English at the New York University Graduate School. He is the author of twenty books and the editor of more than thirty anthologies of literature and literary criticism.

Professor Bloom's works include *Shelley's Mythmaking* (1959), *The Visionary Company* (1961), *Blake's Apocalypse* (1963), *Yeats* (1970), *A Map of Misreading* (1975), *Kabbalah and Criticism* (1975), and *Agon: Towards a Theory of Revisionism* (1982). *The Anxiety of Influence* (1973) sets forth Professor Bloom's provocative theory of the literary relationships between the great writers and their predecessors. His most recent books are *The American Religion* (1992) and *The Western Canon* (1994).

Professor Bloom earned his Ph.D. from Yale University in 1955 and has served on the Yale faculty since then. He is a 1985 MacArthur Foundation Award recipient and served as the Charles Eliot Norton Professor of Poetry at Harvard University in 1987–88. He is currently the editor of the Chelsea House series Major Literary Characters and Modern Critical Views, and other Chelsea House series in literary criticism.

Introduction

HAROLD BLOOM

For an American reader in 1995, exactly a full century after the first publication of *The Red Badge of Courage,* Stephen Crane's short novel is likely to seem far less original than it was and still is. Our novelists of war—Ernest Hemingway and Norman Mailer in particular—absorbed Crane's impressionistic mode of rendering battle, Hemingway directly from Crane, Mailer through Hemingway. Impressionism in *The Red Badge of Courage* has little to do with Impressionist painting, though H. G. Wells affirmed that Crane was more like the expatriate American painter, Whistler, than he was like Tolstoy or Joseph Conrad. Style in Crane's writing is an art of omission, even of the names of his protagonists, so long as he can delay divulging them. The central figure, the Young Soldier, later named as Henry Fleming, is a lens or camera eye whose perceptions and sensations provide all the material that is available to the third-person narrator, who presumably is Stephen Crane himself. We therefore are not given a coherent account of the bloody Civil War battle of Chancellorsville (2–4 May, 1863). You would not know from reading *The Red Badge of Courage* that Robert E. Lee's army won the battle, at the cost of a fatal wound to Stonewall Jackson. Chancellorsville was the last major victory for the Confederacy, and tempted Lee to his invasion of Pennsylvania that ended with the disaster of Pickett's charge at Gettysburg. But none of that is Crane's concern in his impressionistic novel. Like his mentor Tolstoy, Crane knows that battle is a blur to the individual who perceives it. In *War and Peace,* Tolstoy's Pierre observes the crucial, vast fight at Borodino between Napoleon and the Russians, and sees only a senseless chaos. Crane's Henry Fleming also sees only a heap of broken images, fragments of perception, sudden sensations of fear or grotesque visions of a distorted phantasmagoria.

The mind of Henry Fleming, and not the battlefield of Chancellorsville, is the scene of the book, but Fleming's mind is not Crane's subject in the sense that the mind of Hamlet is Shakespeare's. Hamlet's mind is intellectual to the highest degree; his tragedy is the tragedy of thought, of thinking not too much but too well. Henry Fleming's consciousness is painted for us, rather than thought through. Hamlet's intellectual capacities, immense to begin with, grow to infinitude. Henry Fleming, who begins with a limited vision of reality, unable always to distinguish between his perceptions and outer actualities, develops into someone who can trust his own visual impressions. In the context of battle and its fears, such trust is all-important. Whether Fleming, at the close, has evolved into a person of considerable courage, Crane leaves somewhat unclear. Whatever Crane's intentions, the irony of his style continues: "He had been to touch the great death, and found that, after all, it was but the great death. He was a man." I once rephrased that as: "He had been to touch the great fear, and found that, after all, it was still the great fear. He was not yet a man." Which is to say that, the fear of being afraid dehumanizes one, but to accept one's own mortality joins one with one's comrades. Such a joining with others restores the sense of humanity that makes Fleming one of us, all condemned men and women but with a kind of indefinite reprieve. Crane does not wish us to see Fleming as a potential war hero or even as a survivor. The Young Soldier is an Everyman, making a pilgrim's progress into reality, and the name of the reality principle is the necessity of dying.

Henry Fleming, when we last see him, has raised himself to the fury of battle, but still lacks the self-possession of Jim Conklin, the perhaps Christ-like figure of heroism who truly wears the red badge of courage. Fleming's fury, which sustains him in battle, is hardly Crane's conception of courage. Clearsightedness is; Henry is both angry and visually perceptive at the close, which is evidently an ambiguity that the always-ironic Crane sought to establish. For Crane, consistency is impossible, whether in battle or in ordinary life. Heroism is possible, but is bound to be confused with rage, and cannot persist even as a level perception of reality. Crane was so pervasive an ironist that he did not exempt himself as writer from the dilemmas of fear and courage shading into one another. The author's stance in *The Red Badge of Courage* strives for a detachment that Crane knows he cannot attain. In this regard, Crane is closer to Norman Mailer than to Hemingway, who invested himself in the beautiful detachment of his prose, and sometimes deceived himself into believing that he had reached a Tolstoyan eminence of being able to render the completeness of ordinary reality. Crane seems to have known better; the impressionism of *The Red Badge of Courage* is not so much an ambitious attempt at modern epic as it is an honest acceptance of Crane's limitations. He was too aware of his own mortality to escape an ironic stance; tubercular, he died at twenty-eight, just five years after *The Red Badge of Courage* was published. Readers tend to agree that the book's permanent greatness has more to do with its clear-sightedness than with its ironies. ❖

Biography of
Stephen Crane

Stephen Crane was born in Newark, New Jersey, on November 1, 1871, the fourteenth and last child (of whom nine survived to adulthood) of the Rev. Dr. Jonathan Townley Crane and Mary Helen Peck Crane. In his early years Crane chafed at being labeled a "preacher's son," and the rebelliousness he gained in youth persisted throughout his short life. In 1878 his family moved to Port Jervis, a small town in New York near the intersection of New York, New Jersey, and Pennsylvania; it would later become the "Whilomville" of Crane's short stories. Two years later his father died, and in 1883 Crane's mother moved the family to Asbury Park, New Jersey.

Crane enrolled at the Hudson River Institute, a military prep school at Claverack, New York, in 1888. He then attended Lafayette College (1890) and Syracuse University (1891), both of which he left without taking a degree. At Syracuse he began doing some newspaper work, and after leaving the college he went to New York to work as a journalist, first with the *New York Tribune* and later with the *New York Herald.* He was, however, not successful as a reporter, irritated at the mundane tasks assigned him and yearning for more in-depth reporting duties. Living in great poverty in the slums of New York, Crane published the first several of his "Sullivan County Sketches" in 1892, also producing a draft of a novel, *Maggie: A Girl of the Streets.* Rejected by many publishers, the novel was finally printed privately at his own expense in 1893, but it sold very poorly.

In 1894 Crane suddenly began writing free verse of a grim, cynical, and philosophical sort; he might perhaps have been inspired by William Dean Howells's reports of reading the poetry of Emily Dickinson. In 1895 his first volume of verse, *The Black Riders and Other Lines,* appeared. In an attempt to make money, Crane decided to write a swashbuckling romance of Civil War times for popular consumption; but this work was metamorphosed into *The Red Badge of Courage,* widely hailed as a masterpiece of psychological realism. Partial literary inspiration for the work may have come from Crane's friendship with Howells and Hamlin Garland, two leading realist writers of the period. The novel was first published in an abridged form in many newspapers (750 by one count) across the country, then in book form in the fall of 1895. It brought Crane instant international celebrity.

In early 1895 Crane headed west as a reporter for the Bacheller Syndicate, traveling to St. Louis, New Orleans, Nebraska (where he talked with the young Willa Cather), Mexico, Arizona, and Nevada. The next year Crane—who had had a succession of infatuations with women in his early twenties—became involved with several women, although he apparently did not engage in sexual relations with any of them. One of these was Nellie Crouse, to whom he wrote many love letters. Another was Dora Clark, whose arrest on what he believed to be a false charge of solicitation Crane attempted to prevent. Newspapers picked up on the story and sensationalized it, and Crane's reputation was significantly damaged in the process. Crane published two poorly received novels at this time, *George's Mother* (1896), a story of slum life, and *The Third Violet* (1897), a tale about art students.

Later in 1896 Crane went to Jacksonville, Florida, to report on the war in Cuba. Here he met Cora Taylor, the owner of a nightclub and whorehouse who became his common-law wife (she was still married to, but separated from, her second husband). On January 2, 1897, he was aboard the *Commodore* when it sank off the Florida coast. Crane was reported by many newspapers as having drowned, but he had managed to sail to shore on a dinghy. He later wrote up this episode in fictional form in the short story "The Open Boat." Later that year he traveled to Greece to report on the Turkish war (which would serve as the setting for his novel *Active Service,* 1899), then went to England, where he developed a close friendship with Joseph Conrad, to whom his work is often compared, and Harold Frederic, who had written a glowing tribute to him upon the publication of *The Red Badge of Courage.*

Crane returned to the United States in April 1898, as the Spanish-American War broke out. He volunteered for military service but was rejected because of signs of tuberculosis.

Instead, he became a war correspondent for the *New York World* and sent home some of the war's best dispatches from the front, before his increasing illness forced him to return to New York late in 1898. During Christmas week of 1899 Crane suffered a massive tubercular hemorrhage; Cora Taylor then took him to Badenweiler, Germany, in a desperate attempt to restore his health. Crane died on June 5, 1900, almost immediately after his arrival in Germany.

Among Crane's other works published before or just after his death are another collection of free verse, *War Is Kind* (1899); the short story collections *The Open Boat and Other Tales of Adventure* (1898), *The Monster and Other Stories* (1899), and *Whilomville Stories* (1900); two collections of sketches, *The Little Regiment and Other Episodes of the American Civil War* (1896) and *Great Battles of the World* (1901); and a romantic adventure novel, *The O'Ruddy* (1903), left unfinished at his death and completed by Robert Barr. Crane's *Letters* were published in 1960, in an edition prepared by R. W. Stallman and Lillian Gilkes. A critical edition of his *Works* has been prepared by Fredson Bowers (10 vols., 1969–76).

In recent years a controversy has emerged over which text of *The Red Badge of Courage* is to be regarded as definitive. Hershel Parker and Henry Binder have contended that an earlier draft of the novel—in which the author treated his protagonist Henry Fleming with much greater irony—is Crane's preferred text and that he was forced by his publisher, D. Appleton & Company, to abridge and alter the work. Other scholars dispute this claim, and at least two competing versions of *The Red Badge of Courage* are currently available, as well as the newspaper abridgment of 1894. ❖

Thematic and
Structural Analysis

Chapter one of *The Red Badge of Courage* establishes two major themes. The first is in the continual movement and change in the natural world juxtaposed with the movement and actions of an army regiment. Cold, fog, and darkness depart and the army awakens. The movement into spring, as the movement of the army into battle, suggests cyclical events. The road is a symbol that suggests a second theme, that this will be an initiation story, a movement toward the fulfillment of some destiny. The cold sleep of winter and the "eagerness" of inactive soldiers signify a movement into change and experience. In an impressionistic style (presenting a character's subjective impressions rather than an objective reality) the narrator hints at perceptive limits in the "low brows of distant hills." The second paragraph develops further the theme of limited vision and the unreliability of the characters' evaluations of their own actions.

A "certain tall soldier" who has "developed virtues" returns from washing his shirt at the river with a rumor that the regiment will be moving into battle the next day. His virtues are, as far as we know, in his own mind and his pride at possessing a potentially true piece of news is enough for him to justify adopting the "important air of a herald." The soldier (later identified as Jim Conklin) is at once credible, because the rumor he carries is likely to be true, and unreliable, because it is a rumor at third hand. The men argue their belief or disbelief. The "loud soldier" (later identified as Wilson) embodies the bravado and "tinsel courage" of a young army private, untested by battle. By the narrative construction of this chapter the reader may expect to see the natural world, the battlefield, and all aspects of community through the limited vision of the novel's young protagonist, Henry Fleming.

A "youthful private," Henry Fleming hears the rumor and retires to his bunk to consider the possibility of battle. We learn of his parting from his mother's farm, the "Greeklike struggles" that had inspired boyish war ardor, his hoped-for capacity for heroism, and his desire to participate in the "great affairs of the earth." Because his lurid visions of glory were confirmed by newspaper reports of daily victories and by the church-bell "voice of the people rejoicing in the night," Henry enlisted in the Union army. We see Henry's parting from his mother through his eyes, and her tears make him "ashamed of his purposes." The narrator's ironic tone emphasizes Henry's self-delusions as he recalls his departure from the seminary, where he and other young enlistees had been "overwhelmed with privileges for all of one afternoon," and the girl he had imagined to be in some romantic perturbation over his heroic risk of life. At every train station on the trip to Washington the regiment is "fed and caressed" until he believes "he must be a hero," although subsequent months of routine camp life have convinced him that he is but part of a "vast blue demonstration."

Untested by battle, Henry suspects that he might run from a confrontation. Jim Conklin admits that he himself might run if the rest of the regiment did, and Henry is somewhat comforted. These shifts in mood from elation to dejection, and from activity to inactivity, characterize Crane's depiction of Henry's psychological processes throughout the novel.

Chapter two focuses upon Henry's psychological state as he anticipates battle. He cannot "calculate" the likelihood of his courage based upon anything he has experienced. He turns to his comrades, looking for someone who may similarly doubt himself. At the same time he fears that an "unscrupulous confidant" might betray him. We rarely see Henry through the eyes of his comrades, but instead through his own thoughts and actions as he perceives them. He compares his emotions to those he observes in the other men and becomes "despondent and sullen," convinced that he is the only potential coward. He is a "mental outcast," alone in the "monotony of his suffering."

In **chapter three** the regiment moves toward battle. As their marching becomes more uncomfortable the men discard their knapsacks and the "thick shirts" brought from home, signifying another step in this ritual of initiation. Henry expects the enemy to attack them at any moment, and his heightened state of fear contrasts the regiment's encounter with some "perambulating veterans" who note their as yet undiminished numbers and new uniforms with amusement. By never naming the destination or projecting the duration of their march, Crane stresses the limitations of Henry's point of view. Relieved of their knapsacks, their comforts and burdens from home, the regiment moves quickly toward battle.

The interweaving of the youth's sensory impressions of the natural world with his emotional state characterizes Crane's impressionistic style. "Inclosed" within his own moving regiment, Henry joins a mythic scene where regiments, entering into sunlight, "burst into view like armed men just born of the earth." In this impossible context Henry muses that he is "about to be measured." Torn between an urge to flee and an intense curiosity, he watches a distant skirmish and has time to "probe his sensations." The landscape, a distant house, the woods, all seem threatening to him—he wants to warn his comrades that the generals are "stupids." Typically, this mood is juxtaposed with a period of inactivity in which Henry reflects that both the landscape and his fears of "stupidity and incompetence" have become familiar and, therefore, manageable.

In Henry Fleming's first encounter with the enemy his suspicions of his own weakness are confirmed. **Chapters four, five, and six** describe his sensory impressions of battle and the "war atmosphere" as they enter his fragmented consciousness. Before the new regiment can see the battle they meet the din of exploding shells, the yells of their own retreating troops, and the "horizontal flashes" of artillery in the smoke. The atmosphere of war is terrifying and the "battle reflection that shone for an instant in the faces on the mad current made the youth feel that forceful hands from heaven would not have been able to have held him in place if he could have got intelligent control of his legs." Henry's fear is palpable and not unreasonable. Characteristic of Crane's psychological realism and the theme of movement between past and present, inaction and action, before the enemy comes close Henry recalls a circus parade and "a thousand details of color and form." Spontaneously he fires and becomes part of the "common personality" of the regiment. In his "battle sleep" he is like a "driven beast" focused upon the destruction of the enemy. As he becomes aware of individuals around him and as the battle subsides he notices "a singular absence of heroic poses" among the officers, isolated incidents of death and wounding, the grotesque postures of the dead, and the oratorical quality of distant artillery. He is astonished that Nature has remained tranquil. The battle subsides and he experiences an "ecstasy of self-satisfaction" that abruptly ceases as the enemy returns. Finally overwhelmed and exhausted, he runs "like a rabbit." Henry rationalizes his desertion by asserting to himself that no defense was possible and that he had acted upon his "superior perceptions and knowledge." He is amazed when he overhears officers at the rear exclaim that the line had held. They had won after all.

Chapter seven begins an interlude in which Henry, walking as far as possible from the sounds of battle, contemplates the degree of his guilt. He imagines himself in affinity with the natural "law" that affirms his running from peril. Nature, like his mother, is "a woman with a deep aversion to tragedy" and composes a "religion of peace." But a chapel of "arching boughs" hold the gruesome corpse of a soldier and Henry is terrified. The sounds of Nature seem to hush as the sounds of battle come nearer and he runs toward the "ear-shaking thunder." He walks through a field of corpses to the lines of the wounded moving away from the battle. Here the "tattered soldier" asks, "Where yeh hit?" and Henry is ashamed.

As **chapter nine** begins Henry envies the wounded and wishes only that he had their "red badge of courage," the bloody bandage that signifies initiation into this fraternity of men. He recognizes the "spectral soldier" accompanying him like a "stalking reproach" as Jim Conklin, and his devotion to his friend interrupts his fear of discovery as a coward. The dying soldier's vision is more limited than Henry's—"fixed upon the unknown" he moves with a "mysterious purpose." The "tattered soldier" joins them and they follow Jim into a field where Henry watches, entranced by the agony of his friend's death, this "ceremony" of a "mad religion." The chapter concludes in a famous and disturbing image that suggests Jim Conklin's Christ-like significance and a religious communion: "The red sun was pasted in the sky like a wafer."

In **chapter ten** the mortally wounded "tattered soldier" continues to follow Henry, continually asking where his wound is located. Unwittingly, he shames and enrages Henry, and in revenge the youth abandons him, delirious and dying, in the field. Henry envies the dead who are beyond reproach, whose secrets may no longer be probed.

Fear is the emotion through which Henry perceives his surroundings in **chapter eleven**. He rationalizes his desertion in the spectacle of "terror-stricken wagons" and other men retreating. His fear is vindicated by theirs. His elation is replaced by dejection as a column of infantry appears, moving quickly in the opposite direction toward the battle. They are heroes and "chosen beings" as different from himself as if they carried "weapons of flame and banners of sunlight." Self-pity turns to envy as he pictures himself leading "lurid charges" after which his comrades would contemplate the "magnificent pathos of his dead body." Inspired by his own visions Henry considers returning to the front, but certain difficulties dull his war ardor. He has no gun, he cannot find his regiment, he fears someone would ask for an explanation of his return, and his physical exhaustion had become overwhelming. In his despair and self-loathing he hopes the army will suffer defeat and thereby vindicate his desertion. A moral vindication would make him a "prophet," a "seer" who had perceived the truth of the situation and had wisely run. In his heart he could remain despicable but in the eyes of other men he could not endure the dishonor. He stays near to the battle hoping that, in the inevitable defeat, he may join the retreating "men of courage" and appear as one of them. Concluding that the army will not be defeated, he imagines his comrade's disbelief and their cruelties toward him. He has already become, in his own mind, "a slang phrase," a synonym for cowardice.

In **chapter twelve** Henry's rumination on the "rules for the guidance of the damned" is interrupted abruptly by the terrified retreat of the army. The boyish form of his fears returns as he imagines the enemy as "dragons" with "invincible strides"— the army about "to be swallowed"—and, again, the "red animal, war, the blood-swollen god." Horrified and amazed he stands in their midst, finally grabbing one man by the arm to question him. The frantic soldier violently swings his rifle into Henry's skull and continues to run. Knocked nearly insensible, Henry assumes a posture reminiscent of Jim Conklin, walking "tall soldier fashion" in search of a place where he might fall in peace. But he keeps moving and the troops and the artillery head past him for the front. His visual perceptions are fragmented and disparate impressions of the chaos disappearing into the "blue haze of evening." His physical pain replaces despair, and his vision turns inward to favorite memories of his mother's cooking and the pleasures of swimming in summer. But weariness supplants all thought until a "cheery voice" offers to walk with him and, as if the man holds "a wand of a magic kind" in the night, he guides Henry back to his regiment.

As he approaches the campfire, in **chapter thirteen**, Henry realizes that he has no strength to prevent the ridicule of his comrades. He considers hiding in the surrounding darkness but fatigue and pain have wasted him. The firelight distorts his perceptions and the moving black shadows are revealed as sleeping men only as he comes nearer. A "black and monstrous figure" of a sentry turns out to be Wilson, the "loud soldier." Henry claims to have been shot, presumably by the enemy. A corporal examines the wound and remarks with unwitting irony, " 'Yeh've been grazed by a ball. It's raised a queer lump jest as if some feller had lammed yeh on th' head with a club.' "

In a period of solitude and rest things around him begin to assume various shapes. In the firelight the men appear as if drunk, in assorted positions and aspects of exhaustion. Asleep in the "low-arched hall" of the forest, the soldiers are as ancient companions who some "ethereal wanderer" might believe had spent themselves in drunken celebration. Although Henry does not imagine his comrades as heroes, they are closer to the heroic than he.

In **chapter fourteen** the "hall of the forest" becomes a "charnel palace" in the confusion of his just-awakened mind. In this chapter his interpretative vision moves closer to maturity and Crane continues the theme of opposition between private thought and public action. The "heraldic wind" of the new day is quickly altered by the grim and ceaseless noise of battle. Henry imagines the sleeping men as corpses but quickly realizes that his grim vision is false. Wilson continues to supervise his recovery, and Henry is astonished at the maturity and composure his friend has achieved since their earlier camp life. Henry wonders "where had been born these new eyes" of the former "blatant child" of "tinsel courage." Unlike his friend, Henry cannot yet perceive himself in the context of the war. Wilson remarks that the regiment seemed to have lost over half its men the day before, but that they keep drifting in, just as Henry has. Henry construes this as a dangerous observation and attempts to achieve some psychological advantage over his friend in chapter fifteen.

In the **next two chapters** Henry constructs a version of his past actions from what he imagines is a more heroic point of view. In contrast to Wilson who, in mistaken anticipation of his own death, had given him letters and keepsakes to deliver to relatives, Henry had kept his own fears secret. Because Henry's desertion is unknown to anyone else, only his own thoughts undermine his "self-pride." He had "performed his mistakes in the dark, so he was still a man" and the dragons of war, like the consequences of wrong action, may be escaped after all. More than this, he surmises, his survival suggests that he may be "chosen of the gods and doomed to greatness." Wilson interrupts his daydream to request the return of his letters. Henry complies with magnificent condescension and returns to his "battle pictures" and tales of war in which he may figure himself a hero. Unlike the modest and realistic Wilson, Henry's war experiences have not yet shaped his character. The stress of his intense fear of both battle and discovery overwhelms his vision, and battle pictures are his continual refuge.

In **chapter sixteen** the regiment has arrived at a foggy battlefield. Voices "thud" in the fog and the dull "popping" of guns contrasts the incessant roar of guns and cannons to one side of them. Amidst this din and the obscuring fog the men seem to abandon hope, although they cannot quite imagine defeat. As the sun burns off the fog, Henry is still under the spell of his battle pictures, but they have begun to move him to action. He becomes enraged by the sight of the enemy troops and surprises himself by asserting his regiment's valor. He blames the generals for the continued life of the enemy, which emphasizes his limited perspective on the action. He knows not where he is, nor the dimensions of the battle, nor the movements of any other troops, nor his objective in battle save to move forward until the action ceases. Henry's greatest fear is that his desertion may be revealed. Collective exhaustion binds the men together and takes Henry's mind off his internal struggle, as another battle begins.

In the intensity of battle depicted in **chapters seventeen through nineteen** Henry Fleming achieves a more mature kind of vision. At one moment he imagines himself describing battle pictures to an admiring audience or in serious war discussions with "proved men" like himself, but the next moment the approaching conflict forces these thoughts from his mind and a war rage possesses him. He fires at the enemy as if his shots were his fist landing a fierce blow. In the eyes of his comrades, he becomes a "war devil" and a hero. But Henry had been unaware of this effect upon others. He had fought like "a pagan who defends his religion," and in the process he had displaced his crippling fear and shame.

During a lull in the battle Henry and Wilson collect canteens and search, unsuccessfully, for a stream. Away from their battle position they have a more comprehensive view. Significantly, the road behind their own troops is full of other troops in retreat. When they overhear an officer refer to their regiment as "mule drivers" they are astonished, and more astonished to learn that, within a few minutes, they will charge the enemy. By this new perspective upon himself in the eyes of others Henry had been "made aged. New eyes were given him" and he perceives his insignificance in the events at hand. The friends return to the regiment with their news and the officers direct them into position. A man nearby remarks, "We'll git swallowed": the friends nod in agreement, and the line of men moves into the charge.

Henry responds, unconsciously, and runs directly toward the place where he perceives the enemy to be, through bullets, exploding shells, and the bodies of his fallen comrades. In a moment of epiphany, a moment of profound revelation, Henry's vision becomes more acute. Blades of grass, the air itself, the texture of trees, the men—"all were comprehended."

The "delirium" of men in battle is a "sublime absence of selfishness" that subsides into caution as energy diminishes. "They were become men again."

Henry stays near the flag during the regiment's next movement into battle. The flag has qualities of religious and magical significance: it is a goddess—a woman who calls to him in "the voice of his own hopes"—a talisman that he invests with the power to save his life. The shirt carried "bannerlike" by Jim Conklin in chapter one is replaced by a "creation of beauty and invulnerability," a symbol of redemption, of atonement, in chapter nineteen. This follows Crane's theme of maturity as denoted by a movement from lesser to greater vision. Henry and Wilson wrest the falling flag from the dead color sergeant's grip in "an instant of time." The compressed time of war experience intensifies the cycles between action and inaction, valor and cowardice, that mark a soldier's initiation into war.

"Where in hell yeh goin?" the lieutenant yells as the two friends continue, unaware of the retreat of their depleted and dejected regiment. Henry takes sole possession of the flag, but its power is inactive in him now and he is ashamed of their retreat. He dreams of revenge upon the officers who called them "mule drivers" and feels irrational and murderous. His pride is no longer inspired by fear—and another battle begins.

As Henry waits for the force of the battle to reach him the reader may be struck by the realization that, as color bearer, he cannot both fire a rifle and hold the flag. By this circumstance Crane seems to affirm the youth's confidence in the symbol of valor as a mark of his progress toward maturity. Henry is an unarmed observer of the battle, gratified by the "wolflike temper" of his fighting comrades. A "tableau" of corpses and smoke is a battle picture that all the men see as if from the same perspective. They fight well and restore their pride. The cycle of action and inaction, conflict and rest, repeats, and once more "they were men."

The men return to their own lines in **chapter twenty-one**, and Henry is astonished at the "trivial" distances the battle had covered and by the nearness and short duration of the battle. "He wonders at the number of emotions and events that had been crowded into such little spaces." Crane emphasizes the compression of time and experience in war. Henry is much satisfied with his own performance in these events, particularly with the actions that had moved unconsciously into his experience.

In **chapter twenty-two** Henry records the battle scene like a camera. Crane describes the chaos of the battlefield, on which several skirmishes occur at once, in impressionistic detail. For the first time Henry seems aware that there is some purpose in the war greater than these small battles. In one place two regiments are equally matched in fierce "game." At another scene a "jaunty" brigade emerges from a "yelling wood." Henry is "tranquil," aloof, and "deeply absorbed as a spectator" of the events around him. In this chapter Crane evokes the fantastic images of Henry's earlier fear. The "redoubtable dragons" and the "red animal, the blood-swollen god" are refigured as a "spray of light forms" moving like hounds to capture a "mouthful of prisoners." The flags of enemies appear to be "shaking with laughter," or to move "like crimson foam." The flag Henry carries hangs over him, as still as he, as if of the same mind. Perhaps he was correct in his belief in the magical power of that symbol to save lives.

The lieutenant releases a plethora of oaths and expletives at the men, and events begin to filter through Henry's consciousness. The regiment repels the enemy in "stressed silence." Henry recalls the officers who called them "mule drivers" and "mud diggers," and the intensity of his bitterness paralyzes him, as if he were a child. Hatred and the desire for "absolute revenge" consume him, and he imagines this fulfilled "by his dead body lying, torn and gluttering, upon the field." They would be sorry, he thinks, if he were dead.

Henry becomes once more aware of individual men. A sergeant passes with a ghastly wound to the face; the wounded stir; the dead lie in "impossible shapes"; Wilson and the lieutenant are unhurt, the latter still cursing. But the battle is not over, and Henry's battle pictures have become increasingly fragmented.

In **chapter twenty-three** Henry is a veteran soldier. Ordered to charge the enemy yet again, he calculates the possible moves upon the field before them. He concludes that honor requires them to drive the enemy back. Henry leads, carrying the flag and urging the men forward. But the men need no urging and hurl themselves forward with a spirit that he finally understands. He is one of them and feels "joy" that fear no longer keeps him from pursuing the objectives of battle. In this "battle madness" he imagines a blow to the enemy of mythic proportions; but the enemy retreats, with the exception of a small group that possesses the flag.

Henry covets the enemy flag as if it were a "treasure of mythology" and leaps toward it. The scene has the aura of a mythic battle. The wounded and dead appear as if struck by "bolts from the sky." Henry bears his streaming colors forward toward the enemy color bearer, who is mortally wounded and struggling against death to bring his flag to safety. But Wilson, not Henry, reaches the flag first and forces it from the dying soldier's grip. The symbol, the great prize, that had occupied the "gaze" of Henry's "soul" is won by his friend.

In the **final chapter** Crane's theme of movement and countermovement, of "shot and countershot," shapes Henry Fleming's measure of his own character. The regiment crosses back over the scene of their last charge in order to join with other marching troops. He reflects upon the changes that his experiences have made in him. First, he is glad simply to be alive. He recalls all his actions and finds most satisfying those memories of public deeds that earned the respect of other men. Crane's biblical diction suggests the enormity of Henry's pride: "He saw that he was good." These thoughts are juxtaposed with the memory of his desertion and his cruel abandonment of the "tattered soldier" who had been so selfless despite his own pain, inquiring after Henry's wounds. Self-reproach and the fear of discovery shift toward a more circumspect feeling of shame. At this point of tension between the acts of the hero and the acts of the coward Henry's eyes open to new realizations. The boy of the "earlier gospels" gives way to the man.

In one sense Henry's initiation into manhood is accomplished. But the landscape and the elements evoke the sense of movement and discomfort that characterized the novel's beginning. The rain has made the road a difficult path of "liquid brown mud," pointing toward more crises and a destiny not yet achieved. Henry's self-assurance begins to seem unrealistic when he turns from the "sultry nightmare" of battle pictures to visions of idyllic peace in Nature, and we remember the dead soldier who inhabited such a place, and who casts a shadow upon this image of "soft and eternal peace."

The ending is both equivocal and realistic. Although in some ways a story of moral development, *The Red Badge of Courage* is not a moral tale. Henry never questions the purpose or the justification of this war. Its magnitude extends only as far as he can see. The language of his thoughts changes from mythical to biblical tones, more like the language of his mother and his community, by which Crane reiterates the theme of movement into the past that accompanies the movement into maturity.

Henry's youthful confidence is the more poignant because Crane has shown the constant flux of peace into horror and victory into chaos that constitutes war. And Gettysburg still awaits them all. ❖

—*Tenley Williams*
New York University

List of Characters

Henry Fleming is the protagonist of *The Red Badge of Courage.* Young and inexperienced in the world beyond the farm where he lives with his widowed mother and the town where he has gone to school, he joins the Union army not because of any political passion but to participate in some great action implicit in the myths of warfare that inspired his boyhood fantasies. Henry is a self-absorbed, solipsistic, and unremarkable boy who will be initiated into manhood in the compressed time and intensity of warfare. During the regiment's first skirmish Henry deserts and the rest of the novel pivots upon his fear of discovery and being named a coward by his comrades. Henry is also troubled by his cruel abandonment of the mortally wounded "tattered soldier" after the death of Jim Conklin. Gradually he reconciles his guilt and synthesizes a mature self. He overcomes his fear on the battlefield in acts of unconscious courage that earn him the respect of other men but do not erase his private shame.

After proving his courage with his rifle, Henry takes the flag from the regiment's fallen color sergeant and thereafter enters into battle armed only with this symbol of mythic power and ideal action. He bears the flag heroically in the eyes of other men as he continues to defy his paralyzing fear of battle. Privately, his courage compensates, but never completely, for what he considers his failures of character. At the novel's end Henry Fleming has achieved a measure of assurance and has made a sort of exuberant peace with himself. Life is good, he might tell us, and even the beauty of Nature congratulates the brave. But, as he joins the other troops marching toward yet other battles, we may be saddened because we know what he does not—that the worst of the war, and the worst of life, has yet to touch him.

Wilson is identified as the "loud soldier." He is young, brash, and boastful, and his process toward maturity is visible, public. We see him through Henry's eyes and know of him only what Henry knows. Wilson is marked by his trust in the visible character of Henry Fleming. He believes without question Henry's claim to have been wounded in battle, yet he never reveals what particular incident has effected the change in his own character. Wilson's new maturity is marked by solicitude and humility. Henry is not a subtle thinker when it comes to interpreting the actions of others, and Wilson's trust magnifies his despair over his actions and his lie. Wilson's public ingenuousness is the double to Henry's private cowardice.

Wilson takes the enemy flag that Henry covets and appropriates the symbolic measure of his and Henry's progress toward maturity. Both young men have earned the right to carry the symbol of mythic glory and courage. In this they are equals and they become friends.

Jim Conklin signals the protagonist point of view in chapter one. His shirt seems like a flag, and the image foreshadows the development of one of the novel's central tropes. In the novel he functions as a symbol rather than as a character. His acceptance and endurance of great suffering points toward redemption. By his association with Christian imagery at his death Jim confirms the moral teaching of the community that Mrs. Fleming represents amidst Henry's pagan response to myths of ancient war and the pathetic fallacy. ❖

Critical Views

[*The Red Badge of Courage* received generally positive reviews upon its appearance. In this extract, an anonymous reviewer for the *New York Times* praises the work for its realism and for its demolishing of the idea that war is a thing of glory and heroism.]

Stephen Crane is very young—not yet twenty-five, It is said—and this picture he presents of war is therefore a purely imaginative work. The very best thing that can be said about it, though, is that it strikes the reader as a statement of facts by a veteran. ⟨. . .⟩

Probably Mr. Crane has put some of his own mental traits into the composition of his otherwise commonplace hero. Therefore, it is not possible to accept this graphic study of his mind under the stress of new and frightful experiences as an exact picture of the mental states of every green soldier under his first fire. All its complexities are surely not typical.

Yet it is as a picture which seems to be extraordinarily true, free from any suspicion of ideality, defying every accepted tradition of martial glory, that the book commends itself to the reader. The majesty, the pomp and circumstance of glorious war, Mr. Crane rejects altogether. War, as he depicts it, is a mean, nasty, horrible thing; its seeming glories are the results of accident or that blind courage when driven to bay and fighting for life that the meanest animal would show as strongly as man. For it must be remembered that the point of view is consistently that of the humblest soldier in the ranks, who never knows where he is going or what is expected of him until the order comes, who never comprehends the whole scheme, but only his small share of it, who is frequently put forward as an intentional sacrifice, but yet is a sentient human being, who is bound to have his own opinions founded on the scanty knowledge he possesses, his own hopes and fears and doubts and prejudices.

Private Henry Fleming goes to the war a hot-headed young patriot with his mind brimful of crude ideas of glory, and a settled conviction that his capacity for heroism is quite out of the common. Weary months of drill in camp reduce him seemingly to the proper machinelike condition. He learns many things, among them that the glories of war have been greatly exaggerated in books, that the enemy is not composed chiefly of bragging cowards, that victory is rare and dear, and that the lot of a private soldier is very hard. On the eve of his first battle he has about abandoned all hope of ever getting a chance to distinguish himself. Yet when the hour comes it brings depression instead of exhilaration. He communes with himself, and fears that he is a coward. ⟨. . .⟩

The book is written in terse and vigorous sentences, but not without some unpleasant affectations of style which the author would do well to correct. His natural talent is so strong that it is a pity its expression should be marred by petty tricks. When he begins a sentence with "too," for instance, he makes a sensitive reader squirm. But he is certainly a young man of remarkable promise.

—Unsigned, "A Green Private under Fire," *New York Times*, 19 October 1895, p. 3

HAROLD FREDERIC ON STEPHEN CRANE'S NEW TECHNIQUE

[Harold Frederic (1856–1898) was an American journalist and novelist who, although spending most of his adult life in England, wrote much about American life in his fiction. His best-known novel is *The Damnation of Theron Ware* (1896), but he also wrote two books about the Civil War, *The Copperhead* (1893) and *Marsena and Other Stories* (1894). He befriended Crane and helped to champion his work in England. In this extract, Frederic recognizes that Crane has done something new in *The Red Badge of Courage* and that

his work is not "realistic" in the conventional sense of
the term.]

If there were in existence any books of a similar character, one
could start confidently by saying that it was the best of its kind.
But it has no fellows. It is a book outside of all classification. So
unlike anything else is it, that the temptation rises to deny that
it is a book at all. When one searches for comparisons, they can
only be found by culling out selected portions from the trunks
of masterpieces, and considering these detached fragments,
one by one, with reference to the *Red Badge*, which is itself a
fragment, and yet is complete. Thus one lifts the best battle
pictures from Tolstoï's great *War and Peace*, from Balzac's
Chouans, from Hugo's *Les Miserables*, and the forest fight in
'*93*, from Prosper Mérimée's assault of the redoubt, from
Zola's *La Débacle* and *Attack on the Mill*, (it is strange enough
that equivalents in the literature of our own language do not
suggest themselves,) and studies them side by side with this
tremendously effective battle painting by the unknown youngster. Positively they are cold and ineffectual beside it. The
praise may sound exaggerated, but really it is inadequate.
These renowned battle descriptions of the big men are made to
seem all wrong. The *Red Badge* impels the feeling that the
actual truth about a battle has never been guessed before. ⟨. . .⟩

The central idea of the book is of less importance than the
magnificent graft of externals upon it. We begin with the
young raw recruit, hearing that at last his regiment is going to
see some fighting, and brooding over the problem of his own
behavior under fire. We follow his perturbed meditations
through thirty pages which cover a week or so of this menace
of action. Then suddenly, with one gray morning, the ordeal
breaks abruptly over the youngster's head. We go with him, so
close that he is never out of sight, for two terribly crowded
days, and then the book is at an end. This cross-section of his
experience is made a part of our own. We see with his eyes,
think with his mind, quail or thrill with his nerves. He strives to
argue himself into the conventional soldier's bravery; he runs
ingloriously away; he excuses, defends, and abhors himself in
turn; he tremblingly yields to the sinister fascination of creep-
ing near the battle; he basely allows his comrades to ascribe to

heroism the wound he received in the frenzied "sauve qui peut" of the fight, he gets at last the fire of combat in his veins, and blindly rushing in, deports himself with such hardy and temerarious valor that even the Colonel notes him, and admits that he is a "jimhickey." These sequent processes, observed with relentless minutiae, are so powerfully and speakingly portrayed that they seem the veritable actions of our own minds. To produce this effect is a notable triumph, but it is commonplace by comparison with the other triumph of making us realize what Henry saw and heard as well as what he felt. The value of the former feat has the limitations of the individual. No two people are absolutely alike; any other young farm boy would have passed through the trial with something different somewhere. Where Henry fluttered, he might have been obtuse; neither the early panic nor the later irrational ferocity would necessarily have been just the same. But the picture of the trial itself seems to me never to have been painted as well before.

⟨. . .⟩ When Warren Lee Goss began his *Personal Recollections of a Private,* his study of the enlistment, the early marching and drilling, and the new experiences of camp life was so piquant and fresh that I grew quite excited in anticipation. But when he came to the fighting, he fell flat. The same may be said, with more reservations, about the first parts of Judge Tourgée's more recent *Story of a Thousand.* It seems as if the actual sight of a battle has some dynamic quality in it which overwhelms and crushes the literary faculty in the observer. At best, he gives us a conventional account of what happened; but on analysis, you find that this is not what he really saw, but what all his reading has taught him that he must have seen. In the same way battle painters depict horses in motion, not as they actually move, but as it has been agreed by numberless generations of draughtsmen to say that they move. At last, along comes a Muybridge, with his instantaneous camera, and shows that the real motion is entirely different.

It is this effect of a photographic revelation which startles and fascinates one in *The Red Badge of Courage.* The product is breathlessly interesting, but still more so is the suggestion behind it that a novel force has been disclosed, which may do all sorts of other remarkable things. Prophecy is known of old as a tricky and thankless hag, but all the same I cannot close my ears to her hint that a young man who can write such a first book as that will make us all sit up in good time.

—Harold Frederic, "Stephen Crane's Triumph," *New York Times*, 26 January 1896, p. 22

A. C. McClurg on Crane's Inaccuracies

[A. C. McClurg (1832–1901) entered the Civil War on the Union side as a private and left as a colonel, distinguishing himself in several important battles. He was later made a brigadier-general, but he left the military and went into the bookselling business, ultimately founding the publishing company that bears his name and publishing the significant literary journal, the *Dial* (1880–1929). In this extract, McClurg is deeply offended at the ironic view of the Civil War (and, implicitly, of the men at the top of the military hierarchy) in Crane's novel, feeling it to be an inaccurate portrayal of how the war was actually conducted.]

Must we come to judge of books only by what the newspapers have said of them, and must we abandon all the old standards of criticism? Can a book and an author, utterly without merit, be puffed into success by entirely undeserved praise, even if that praise come from English periodicals?

One must ask these questions after he has been seduced into reading a book recently reprinted in this country entitled *The Red Badge of Courage, an Episode of the American Civil War.* The chorus of praise in the English papers has been very extravagant, but it is noticeable that so far, at least, the American papers have said very little about the merits or demerits of the book itself. They simply allude to the noise made over it abroad, and therefore treat its author as a coming factor in our literature. Even *The Dial's* very acute and usually very discerning critic of contemporary fiction (Mr. Payne) treats the book and the author (in your issue of Feb. 1) in very much this way— that is, as a book and an author to be reckoned with, not because of any good which he himself finds in them, but because they have been so much talked about.

The book has very recently been reprinted in America, and would seem to be an American book, on an American theme, and by an American author, yet originally issued in England. If it is really an American production one must suppose it to have been promptly and properly rejected by any American publishers to whom it may have been submitted, and afterward more naturally taken up by an English publisher.

It is only too well known that English writers have had a very low opinion of American soldiers, and have always, as a rule, assumed to ridicule them. ⟨. . .⟩

Under such circumstances we cannot doubt that *The Red Badge of Courage* would be just such a book as the English would grow enthusiastic over, and we cannot wonder that the redoubtable *Saturday Review* greeted it with the highest encomiums, and declared it the actual experiences of a veteran of our War, when it was really the vain imaginings of a young man born long since that war, a piece of intended realism based entirely on unreality. The book is a vicious satire upon American soldiers and American armies. The hero of the book (if such he can be called—"the youth" the author styles him) is an ignorant and stupid country lad, who, without a spark of patriotic feeling, or even of soldierly ambition, has enlisted in the army from no definite motive that the reader can discover, unless it be because other boys are doing so; and the whole book, in which there is absolutely no story, is occupied with giving what are supposed to be his emotions and his actions in the first two days of battle. His poor weak intellect, if indeed he has any, seems to be at once and entirely overthrown by the din and movement of the field, and he acts throughout like a madman. Under the influence of mere excitement, for he does not even appear to be frightened, he first rushes madly to the rear in a crazy panic, and afterward plunges forward to the rescue of the colors under exactly the same influences. In neither case has reason or any intelligent motive any influence on his action. He is throughout an idiot or a maniac, and betrays no trace of the reasoning being. No thrill of patriotic devotion to cause or country ever moves his breast, and not even an emotion of manly courage. Even a wound which he finally gets comes from a comrade who strikes him on the head with his musket to get rid of him; and this is the only *Red Badge of Courage* (!) which we discover in the book. A number of other characters come in to fill out the two hundred and thirty-three pages of the book,—such as "the loud soldier," "the tall soldier," "the tattered soldier," etc., but not one of them betrays any more sense, self-possession, or courage than does "the youth." On the field all is chaos and confusion. "The young lieutenant," "the mounted officer," even "the general," are all utterly demented beings, raving and talking alike in an unintelligible and hitherto unheard-of jargon, rushing about in a very delirium of madness. No intelligent orders are given; no intelligent movements are made. There is no evidence of drill, none of discipline. There is a constant, senseless, and profane babbling going on, such as one could hear nowhere but in a madhouse. Nowhere are seen the quiet, manly, self-respecting, and patriotic men, influenced by the highest sense of duty, who in reality fought our battles.

It can be said most confidently that no soldier who fought in our recent War ever saw any approach to the battle scenes in this book—but what wonder? We are told that it is the work of a young man of twenty-three or twenty-four years of age, and so of course must be a mere work of diseased imagination. And yet it constantly strains after so-called realism. The result is a mere riot of words. ⟨. . .⟩

It is extraordinary that even a prejudiced animus could have led English writers to lavish extravagant praise on such a book; it is still more extraordinary that an attempt should be made to foist it upon the long-suffering American public, and to push it into popularity here. Respect for our own people should have prevented its issue in this country.

There may have been a moderate number of men in our service who felt and acted in battle like those in this book; but of such deserters were made. They did not stay when they could get away: why should they? The army was no healthy place for them, and they had no reason to stay; there was no moral motive. After they had deserted, however, they remained "loud soldiers," energetic, and blatant,—and they are possibly now enjoying good pensions. It must have been some of these fellows who got the ear of Mr. Crane and told him how they felt and acted in battle.

—A. C. McClurg, "The Red Badge of Hysteria," *Dial,* 16 April 1896, pp. 227–28

STEPHEN CRANE ON HIS ORIGINS AS A WRITER

[Stephen Crane never wrote extensively on the genesis of his novel, but in the following letter he gives a brief summary of his origins as a writer and maintains that *The Red Badge of Courage* was born of "pain" and internal conflict.]

I can't do any sort of work that I don't like or don't feel like doing, and I've given up trying to do it. When I was at school few of my studies interested me, and as a result I was a bad scholar. They used to say at Syracuse University, where, by the way, I didn't finish the course, that I was cut out to be a professional base-ball player. And the truth of the matter is that I went there more to play base-ball than to study. I was always very fond of literature, though. I remember when I was eight years old I became very much interested in a child character called, I think, Little Goodie Brighteyes, and I wrote a story then which I called after this fascinating little person. When I was about sixteen I began to write for the New York newspapers, doing correspondence from Asbury Park and other places. Then I began to write special articles and short stories for the Sunday papers and one of the literary syndicates, reading a great deal in the meantime and gradually acquiring a style. I decided that the nearer a writer gets to life the greater he becomes as an artist, and most of my prose writings have been toward the goal partially described by that misunderstood and abused word, realism. Tolstoï is the writer I admire most of all. I've been a free lance during most of the time I have been doing literary work, writing stories and articles about anything under heaven that seemed to possess interest, and selling them wherever I could. It was hopeless work. Of all human lots for a person of sensibility that of an obscure free lance in literature or journalism is, I think, the most discouraging. It was during this period that I wrote *The Red Badge of Courage.* It was an effort born of pain—despair, almost; and I believe that this made it a better piece of literature than it otherwise would have been. It seems a pity that art should be a child of pain, and yet I think it is. Of course we have fine writers who are prosperous and contented, but in my opinion their work would be greater if this were not so. It lacks the sting it would have if written under the spur of a great need.

> —Stephen Crane, Letter to J. Herbert Welch (late April–May 1896), *The Correspondence of Stephen Crane,* ed. Stanley Wertheim and Paul Sorrentino (New York: Columbia University Press, 1988), Vol. 1, pp. 231–32

H. G. WELLS ON CRANE'S LITERARY METHOD

[H. G. Wells (1866–1946), the celebrated novelist and historian, was one of many English writers who praised Crane's work. In this extract, written shortly after Crane's death, Wells draws a provocative analogy between Crane's literary method and painting, introducing the word "impression" and thereby suggesting that Crane's technique is what we now call impressionism.]

Though my personal acquaintance with Crane was so soon truncated, I have followed his work for all the four years it has been known in England. I have always been proud, and now I am glad, that, however obscurely, I also was in the first chorus of welcome that met his coming. It is, perhaps, no great distinction for me; he was abundantly praised; but, at least, I was early and willing to praise him when I was wont to be youthfully jealous of my praises. His success in England began with *The*

Red Badge of Courage, which did, indeed, more completely than any other book has done for many years, take the reading public by storm. Its freshness of method, its vigor of imagination, its force of color and its essential freedom from many traditions that dominate this side of the Atlantic, came—in spite of the previous shock of Mr. Kipling—with a positive effect of impact. It was a new thing, in a new school. When one looked for sources, one thought at once of Tolstoi; but, though it was clear that Tolstoi had exerted a powerful influence upon the conception, if not the actual writing, of the book, there still remained something entirely original and novel. To a certain extent, of course, that was the new man as an individual; but, to at least an equal extent, it was the new man as a typical young American, free at last, as no generation of Americans have been free before, of any regard for English criticism, comment or tradition, and applying to literary work the conception and theories of the cosmopolitan studio with a quite American directness and vigor. For the great influence of the studio on Crane cannot be ignored; in the persistent selection of the essential elements of an impression, in the ruthless exclusion of mere information, in the direct vigor with which the selected points are made, there is Whistler even more than there is Tolstoi in *The Red Badge of Courage.* And witness this, taken almost haphazard:

> At nightfall the column broke into regimental pieces, and the fragments went into the fields to camp. Tents sprang up like strange plants. Camp fires, like red, peculiar blossoms, dotted the night. . . . From this little distance the many fires, with the black forms of men passing to and fro before the crimson rays, made weird and satanic effects.

And here again; consider the daring departure from all academic requirements, in this void countenance:

> A warm and strong hand clasped the youth's languid fingers for an instant, and then he heard a cheerful and audacious whistling as the man strode away. As he who had so befriended him was thus passing out of his life, it suddenly occurred to the youth that he had not once seen his face.

I do not propose to add anything here to the mass of criticism upon this remarkable book. Like everything else which has been abundantly praised, it has occasionally been praised

"all wrong;" and I suppose that it must have been said hundreds of times that this book is a subjective study of the typical soldier in war. But Mr. George Wyndham, himself a soldier of experience, has pointed out in an admirable preface to a reissue of this and other of Crane's war studies, that the hero of the *Red Badge* is, and is intended to be, altogether a more sensitive and imaginative person than the ordinary man. He is the idealist, the dreamer of boastful things brought suddenly to the test of danger and swift occasions and the presence of death.
—H. G. Wells, "Stephen Crane from an English Standpoint," *North American Review* No. 525 (August 1900): 234–35

JOSEPH CONRAD ON CRANE'S DISTINCTIVE STYLE

[The novelist Joseph Conrad (1857–1924) had made Crane's acquaintance when the latter visited England in 1897. In this extract from an introduction to *The Red Badge of Courage,* Conrad maintains that the greatness of Crane's novel is its distinctive style, mingling dignity and colloquialism, as well as the modernism of its approach to war, which foreshadowed the unglamorous horrors of World War I.]

Stephen Crane places his Young Soldier in an untried regiment. And this is well contrived—if any contrivance there be in a spontaneous piece of work which seems to spurt and flow like a tapped stream from the depths of the writer's being. In order that the revelation should be complete, the Young Soldier has to be deprived of the moral support which he would have found in a tried body of men matured in achievement to the consciousness of its worth. His regiment had been tried by nothing but days of waiting for the order to move; so many days that it and the Youth within it have come to think of themselves as merely "a part of a vast blue demonstration." The army had been lying camped near a river, idle and fretting, till the moment when Stephen Crane lays hold of it at dawn with masterly simplicity: "The cold passed reluctantly from the earth. . . ." These are the first words of the war book which was to give him his crumb of fame.

The whole of that opening paragraph is wonderful in the homely dignity of the indicated lines of the landscape, and the shivering awakening of the army at the break of the day before the battle. In the next, with a most effective change to racy colloquialism of narrative, the action which motivates, sustains and feeds the inner drama forming the subject of the book, begins with the Tall Soldier going down to the river to wash his shirt. He returns waving his garment above his head. He had heard at fifth-hand from somebody that the army is going to move tomorrow. The only immediate effect of this piece of news is that a Negro teamster, who had been dancing a jig on a wooden box in a ring of laughing soldiers, finds himself suddenly deserted. He sits down mournfully. For the rest, the Tall Soldier's excitement is met by blank disbelief, profane grumbling, an invincible incredulity. But the regiment is somehow sobered. One feels it, though no symptoms can be noticed. It does not know what a battle is; neither does the Young Soldier. He retires from the babbling throng into what seems a rather comfortable dug-out and lies down with his hands over his eyes to think. Thus the drama begins.

He perceives suddenly that he had looked upon wars as historical phenomenons of the past. He had never believed in war in his own country. It had been a sort of play affair. He had been drilled, inspected, marched for months, till he had despaired "of ever seeing a Greek-like struggle. Such were no more. Men were better or more timid. Secular and religious education had effaced the throat-grappling instinct, or else firm finance held in check the passions."

Very modern this touch. We can remember thoughts like these round about the year 1914. That Young Soldier is representative of mankind in more ways than one, and first of all in his ignorance. His regiment had listened to the tales of veterans, "tales of grey bewhiskered hordes chewing tobacco with unspeakable valour and sweeping along like the Huns." Still, he cannot put his faith in veterans' tales. Recruits were their prey. They talked of blood, fire, and sudden death, but much of it might have been lies. They were in nowise to be trusted. And the question arises before him whether he will or will not "run from a battle"? He does not know. He cannot know. A little panic fear enters his mind. He jumps up and asks himself aloud, "Good Lord! What's the matter with me?" This is the first time his words are quoted, on this day before the battle. He dreads not danger, but fear itself. He stands before the unknown. He would like to prove to himself by some reasoning process that he will not "run from the battle." And in his unblooded regiment he can find no help. He is alone with the problem of courage.

In this he stands for the symbol of all untried men.
—Joseph Conrad, "His War Book" (1925), *Last Essays* (New York: Doubleday, 1926), pp. 121–23

JOHN E. HART ON THE MYTHIC STRUCTURE OF *THE RED BADGE OF COURAGE*

[John E. Hart (b. 1917) is a former professor of English and American literature at Albion College in Albion, Michigan. He has written monographs on Floyd Dell (1971) and Albert Halper (1980). In this extract, Hart believes that *The Red Badge of Courage* operates not by means of conventional realism but by symbol, metaphor, and myth, and that it follows the mythic structure of separation, initiation, and return.]

When Stephen Crane published *The Red Badge of Courage* in 1895, the book created an almost immediate sensation. Crane had had no experience in war, but in portraying the reactions of a young soldier in battle, he had written with amazing accuracy. As one way of re-examining *The Red Badge of Courage,* we would want to read it as myth and symbolic action. Clearly, the construction of the story, its moral and meaning, its reliance on symbol follow in detail the traditional formula of myth. Crane's main theme is the discovery of self, that unconscious self, which, when identified with the inexhaustible energies of the group, enables man to understand the "deep forces that have shaped man's destiny." The progressive movement of the hero, as in all myth, is that of separation, initiation, and return. Within this general framework, Crane plots his story with individual variation. Henry Fleming, a Youth, ventures forth from his known environment into a region of naturalistic, if not super-naturalistic wonder; he encounters the monstrous forces of war and death; he is transformed through a series of rites and revelations into a hero; he returns to identify his new self with the deeper communal forces of the group and to bestow the blessings of his findings on his fellow comrades.

Whatever its "realistic" style, much of the novel's meaning is revealed through the use of metaphor and symbol. The names of characters, for example, suggest both particular attributes and general qualities: the Tall Soldier, whose courage and confidence enable him to measure up to the vicissitudes of war and life; the Loud Soldier, the braggart, the over-confident, whose personality is, like Henry's, transformed in war; the Tattered Soldier, whose clothes signify his lowly and exhausted plight; the Cheery Man, whose keenness and valor prevent his falling into despair. Likewise, the use of color helps to clarify and extend the meaning. Red, traditionally associated with blood and fire, suggests courage, flag, life-energy, desire, ambition. Black, traditionally associated with death, implies "great unknown," darkness, forests, and, by extension, entombment and psychological death. The whole paraphernalia of myth-religious and sacrificial rites—the ceremonial dancing, the dragons with fiery eyes, the menacing landscape, the entombment, the sudden appearance of a guide, those symbols so profoundly familiar to the unconscious and so frightening to the conscious personality—give new dimensions of meaning to the novel.

—John E. Hart, "*The Red Badge of Courage* as Myth and Symbol," *University of Kansas City Review* 19, No. 4 (Summer 1953): 249

[Ralph Ellison (1914–1994), an important black American novelist and author of *Invisible Man* (1952), also wrote a small body of literary criticism. In this extract, Ellison maintains that the true focus of *The Red Badge of Courage* is its depiction of war as an invasion of privacy.]

⟨. . .⟩ for a novel supposedly about the war, *The Red Badge* is intensely concerned with invasion of the private life, a theme announced when the men encounter the body of their first dead soldier, whose shoe soles, "worn to the thinness of writing paper," strike Henry as evidence of a betrayal by fate which in death had exposed to the dead Confederate's enemies "that poverty which in life he had perhaps concealed from his friends." But war is nothing if not an invasion of privacy, and so is death (the "invulnerable" dead man forces his way between the men as they open ranks to avoid him); and society, more so. For society, even when reduced to a few companions, invades personality and demands of the individual an almost impossible consistency while guaranteeing the individual hardly anything. Or so it seems to the naïve Henry, much of whose anguish springs from the fear that his friends will discover that the wound which he received from the rifle butt of another frightened soldier is not the red badge of courage they assume but a badge of shame. Thus the Tattered Soldier's questions as to the circumstance of his injury (really questions as to his moral identity) fill Henry with fear and hostility, and he regards them as

> the assertion of a society that probed pitilessly at secrets until all is apparent. . . . His late companion's chance persistency made him feel that he could not keep his crime [of malingering] concealed in his bosom. It was sure to be brought plain by one of those arrows which cloud the air and are constantly pricking, discovering, proclaiming those things which are willed to be forever hidden. He admitted that he could not defend himself against this agency. It was not within the power of vigilance. . . .

In time Henry learns to act with honor and courage and to perceive something of what it means to be a man, but this perception depends upon the individual fates of those who make up his immediate group; upon the death of Jim Conklin, the most mature and responsible of the men, and upon the Loud Soldier's attainment of maturity and inner self-confidence. But the cost of perception is primarily personal, and for Henry it depends upon the experience of the moral discomfort which follows the crimes of malingering and assuming a phony identity, and the further crime of allowing the voice of conscience, here symbolized by the Tattered Soldier, to wander off and die. Later he acquits himself bravely and comes to feel that he has attained

> a quiet manhood, non-assertive but of sturdy and strong blood. He knew that he would no more quail before his guides wherever they should point. He had been to touch the great death, and found that, after all, it was but the great death. He was a man.

Obviously although Henry has been initiated into the battle of life, he has by no means finished with illusion—but that, too, is part of the human condition.

> —Ralph Ellison, "Stephen Crane and the Mainstream of American Fiction" (1960), *Shadow and Act* (New York: Random House, 1964), pp. 69–70

EDWIN H. CADY ON THE ENDING OF *THE RED BADGE OF COURAGE*

[Edwin H. Cady (b. 1917), formerly Andrew W. Mellon Professor in the Humanities at Duke University, is a widely published literary critic and author of *The Gentleman in America* (1949), *The Light of Common Day: Realism in American Fiction* (1971), and several books on William Dean Howells. In this extract from his monograph on Crane, Cady studies the ending of *The Red Badge of Courage*, showing that the novel concludes in such a way as to let the reader decide what judgment to pass on Henry Fleming's character.]

If style be taken as texture and form as structure, the question of the equal success of the novel's form depends on deciding the much-discussed problem of the ending. Does the novel end well? Does it end or just disappear? Is there a climax? Is the ending of the novel satisfactory, in short, in emphasis and substance?

Debate has raged since the early reviews, and much of it around the last chapter. Though many critics have not troubled to mention it, few would deny the real achievement of a climax in personal victory which comes at the end of the next to the last chapter. Jeered at by veterans, scorned by their general as "mud-diggers" and "mule drivers," barely surviving after a temporary desertion rate of nearly fifty percent on the first day, close to a "pretty success" which they had funked by a hundred feet a little earlier, the regiment had stood exasperatedly under a last pressure. Fleming, now a color-bearer, had resolved "that his final and absolute revenge was to be achieved by his dead body lying, torn and guttering, upon the field." His lieutenant had continued to curse, but it was now "with the air of a man who was using his last box of oaths."

Then the men are ordered to charge and at last, tough, determined, sacrificial, soldier-like, they really do. Fleming forces the way, banner in hand, and Wilson captures the colors of the enemy. There arose "wild clamorings of cheers. The men gesticulated and bellowed in ecstasy." They had even take prisoners. Fleming and Wilson sat "side by side and congratulated each other." The narrative progression has been simple. Beginning in doubt about Fleming's—and the regiment's—courage, it had sunk to despair with his cowardice and Conklin's death. Now it rises to climax in their clear success, even, in a minimal sense, their heroism. The reversed curve is classic. And even more so is the reflective short downward curve of anticlimax at the end as the regiment is recalled and starts to wind its way back over the river and the men can suddenly realize that the battle is over.

As Fleming realizes this, his mind clears of "battle-sleep," and he is able to take stock. Crane trimmed quite a lot from the manuscript of the last chapter, much of it reflecting too exactly the naturalistic debates he also cut. But only one of the cuts was really important. What he was doing with Fleming, it seems clear, was not holding him up for judgment but round-ing off the account of his experience. It was out of the question for Crane, insofar as he was a realist, to end a plot. It was neither with abstract structure nor with fable that he was concerned. The realists saw life as a continuum of the personal experiences of their characters. One broke in upon its flow at one significant point and left it at another. If in the course of this, one had any ulterior ideological motives, they should be planted out of sight and left for the reader to find.

As realist—psychological realist—as impressionist, perhaps even as metaphysician, Crane was, as we have seen, a visionist. The important thing was to see pellucidly and honestly. And what Crane is concerned with at the end of *The Red Badge* is what Fleming can see. By letting the readers see what Fleming sees, Crane will let them decide what to think of him. Henry struggles "to marshal all his acts. . . . From this present point of view he was enabled to look upon them with some correctness, for his new condition had already defeated certain sympathies."

—Edwin H. Cady, *Stephen Crane* (Boston: Twayne, 1962), pp. 140–42

JOHN BERRYMAN ON CRANE'S STYLE

[John Berryman (1914–1972) was a noted American poet—among his volumes of poetry are *Poems* (1942), *The Dispossessed* (1948), and *Homage to Mistress Bradstreet* (1956)—as well as a literary critic. In this extract, Berryman carefully studies the stylistic devices Crane used in *The Red Badge of Courage* to create its impressionistic effect, mingling plainness, poeticism, and restraint.]

This famous style is not easy to describe, combining as it does characteristics commonly antithetical. It is swift, no style in English more so, improvisatorial, manly as Hazlitt; but at the same time it goes in for ritual solemnity and can be highly poetic. I illustrate. For speed: "For a moment he felt in the face of his great trial like a babe, and the flesh over his heart seemed very thin. He seized time to look about him calculatingly." Here we are already into something like the other category, illustrated in the opening sentence of the novel: "The cold passed reluctantly from the earth, and the retiring fogs revealed an army stretched out on the hills, resting." Here's a high case of the animism I have referred to. The colour of the style is celebrated—maybe he got it from a theory of Goethe's; but the style is also plain, plain. Short as it is, it is also unusually iterative; modern and simple, brazen with medieval imagery; animistic, de-human and mechanistic; attentive—brilliantly—to sound: "As he ran, he became aware that the forest had stopped its music, as if at last becoming capable of hearing the foreign sounds. The trees hushed and stood motionless. Everything seemed to be listening to the crackle and clatter and ear-shaking thunder. The chorus pealed over the still earth." Adverbs are used like verbs, word order deformed: somebody leans on a bar and hears other men "terribly discuss a question that was not plain." But the surest attribute of this style is its reserve, as its most celebrated is its colour. Crane guarantees nothing. "Doubtless" is a favorite word. The technique of refusal is brought so far forward that a casual "often" will defeat itself: "What hats and caps were left to them they often slung high in the air." Once more we hear a Shakespearean contempt, as in *Coriolanus.* In a paradoxical way: if he won't vouch for what he tells us—if he doesn't push us, trying to convince—he must have things up his sleeve which if we knew them would persuade us. As for colour: "A crimson roar came from the distance"—the mildest example I have been able to find. His employment of it here is not only not naturalistic—what roar was ever red?—but is solely affective, that is, emotional; like his metaphorical use, in the novel, of devils, ghouls, demons, spectres. Crane made use of a spectrum. A final item is his rueful humour: "He threw aside his mental pamphlets on the philosophy of the retreated and rules for the guidance of the damned."

On that note we might end, except for a poem written by Stephen Crane several years after the novel called "War Is Kind," one of his major poems, and one of the best poems of the period in the United States of America.

In the novel there is little of the pathos of which he had already shown himself a master in *Maggie,* and little of the horror informing his best later war stories. They come to life in the poem. Crane makes a sort of little bridge between Tolstoy—supreme—supreme?—and our very good writer Hemingway. But these superior gentlemen do not compete. One of the best remarks ever made about the poet of the *Iliad* is that he shared with Tolstoy and with Shakespeare both a virile love of war and a virile horror of it. So in his degree did Crane, and before he had seen it.

> —John Berryman, "Stephen Crane: *The Red Badge of Courage*"
> (1965), *The Freedom of the Poet* (New York: Farrar, Straus &
> Giroux, 1976), pp. 175–76

❖

JOHN J. MCDERMOTT ON THE OPENING SCENES OF *THE RED BADGE OF COURAGE*

[John J. McDermott (b. 1932) is a professor of philosophy at Texas A & M University. He has written *The Culture of Experience: Philosophical Essays in the American Grain* (1976) and edited *The Writings of William James* (1967). In this extract, McDermott examines the opening scenes of Crane's novel, which introduce the ironic treatment of war and heroism developed in the rest of the novel.]

In choosing as protagonist for *The Red Badge of Courage* an unsophisticated, inarticulate farm boy, and in attempting convincingly to depict in this protagonist a complicated, only partially rational, psychological change, Stephen Crane obviously set for himself a task of formidable artistic difficulty. One of the devices he uses to overcome this difficulty is the series of thematically related incidents with which he opens his novel. Together these incidents form an appropriate backdrop against which the drama of Henry Fleming's private struggle for manhood may be presented.

A juxtaposition of no more than the title, *The Red Badge of Courage,* and some opening lines of the work indicates that

Crane's novel is enriched with complicating ironies. For the first badge of virtue we see in the novel is a deceptive one: a "tall soldier" (who we later learn is Jim Conklin, the most conventionally courageous soldier in the novel) having "developed virtues," decides, as a first practical result of his new-found virtues, to wash his dirty shirt. While laundering he naively absorbs an inaccurate rumor which he feels compelled to share with his fellows. He then waves his freshly cleaned "bannerlike" shirt aloft and rushes back to camp. There he repeats the tale which he has just heard, only to have it immediately and with partial accuracy identified by one of his listeners as " 'a thunderin' lie!' " Conventional virtue, then, Crane announces as his work opens, may well lead only to trivial actions, and its flaunted banners may herald only partial truths.

The specific virtue of courage in battle is soon introduced in similarly mocking contexts. Even before the battle begins, veteran soldiers tell Henry Fleming that the enemy may be advancing while "chewing tobacco with unspeakable valor." As the army moves to a confrontation with the enemy, Bill Smithers, one of the men in Henry's regiment, stumbles and falls, and as he lies sprawling one of his own comrades treads on his hand. We later learn Smithers has three fingers crushed so badly by this accident that a doctor wants to amputate them. But at the time of the trampling the rest of the men in the ranks merely laugh as Smithers swears in pain, the first among them to be wounded. And as the regiment continues its march toward the battle lines the men satirically cheer the first opponent they encounter, a "dauntless" young girl who fights with a fat private for possession of her horse: "They jeered the piratical private, and called attention to various defects in his personal appearance; and they were wildly enthusiastic in support of the young girl." So Crane skillfully dramatizes an external reality which challenges the simpleminded notions of heroism which his naive protagonist has brought with him to the army.

—John J. McDermott, "Symbolism and Psychological Realism in *The Red Badge of Courage*," *Nineteenth-Century Fiction* 23, No. 3 (December 1968): 324–25

[Robert M. Rechnitz is a professor of English at
Monmouth College in West Long Branch, New Jersey.
In this extract, Rechnitz discusses Henry Fleming's
return to his regiment at the beginning of the second
half of *The Red Badge of Courage,* showing that
Fleming's loyalty to the regiment is qualified by the
realization that many of his fellow soldiers are both lit-
erally and spiritually doomed.]

With Henry's return at the beginning of the second half of the
novel, the dominant motif, that archetypal American movement of alternating escape and return, is several times repeat-
ed, even though there is no possibility of any genuine escape.
The attempted escapes, however, are no longer physical;
rather, they become a matter of allegiances and commitments.
When Henry's individuality dominates, he curses the army. As
the novel moves closer to its conclusion, he identifies increasingly with the army.

Quite understandably, Henry's initial loyalty upon returning
is to the regiment. Wounded and exhausted, he sees in the fig-
ures of the sleeping men an image of content, and after having
his wound dressed he sleeps among his comrades. But in
chapter 14 he awakes: "He believed for an instant that he was
in the house of the dead, and he did not dare to move lest
these corpses start up, squalling and squawking." Only a
moment passes before he realizes that "this somber picture
was not a fact of the present, but a mere prophecy." The
prophecy is accurate on two levels: first, of course, many of the
men will be killed in the forthcoming skirmishes. But, second,
the men are all doomed to die in a spiritual sense as they surrender themselves more and more to the demands of the
army.

With some sort of recognition of this second meaning, Henry
is unwilling to accept the officers' leadership. At the beginning
of the new day's combat, furious at the evidence of the Union
defeat, Henry cries out, " 'B'jiminey, we're generaled by a lot 'a
lunkheads.' " Wilson, however in terms reminiscent of Jim

Conklin's, defends the commanding general: " 'Mebbe, it wa'n't all his fault—not all together. He did th' best he knowed. It's our luck t' git licked often,' said his friend in a weary tone. He was trudging along with stooped shoulders and shifting eyes like a man who has been caned and kicked." Wilson may have the better of the argument, but he is a beaten man. The great cost of what we may call his collective vision is but partially revealed in this passage.

It is more fully revealed as further instances of the collective vision are disclosed. In the following action, "deeply absorbed as a spectator," Henry observed the battle:

> The regiment bled extravagantly. Grunting bundles of blue began to drop. The orderly sergeant of the youth's company was shot through the cheeks. Its supports being injured, his jaw hung afar down, disclosing in the wide cavern of his mouth a pulsing mass of blood and teeth. And with it all he made attempts to cry out. In his endeavor there was a dreadful earnestness, as if he conceived that one great shriek would make him well.

Though the events being described here are horrible, the style drains them of emotional content. This is precisely the cost of the collective vision—affectlessness. Throughout the novel, Crane's famous irony insists upon the unspeakable lesson: as he continues to surrender his autonomy to the overwhelming pressure of collectivization, modern man will most likely lose even the capacity to feel.

—Robert M. Rechnitz, "Depersonalization and the Dream in *The Red Badge of Courage*," *Studies in the Novel* 6, No. 1 (Spring 1974): 81–82

FRANK BERGON ON THE AMBIGUOUS ENDING OF CRANE'S NOVEL

[Frank Bergon, a professor of English at Vassar College, is the editor of *A Sharp Lookout: Selected Nature Essays of John Burroughs* (1987) and *The Journals of*

Lewis and Clark (1989) and author of *Stephen Crane's Artistry* (1975), from which the following extract is taken. Here, Bergon studies the ending of *The Red Badge of Courage* in both its original and revised state, finding ambiguity in the final impression the reader is to have of Henry Fleming: Has the war experience changed him permanently or only temporarily?]

At the end of the novel Fleming is certainly a "man" in the sense that he is no longer a savage beast, but his idea of being a man seems grander than his just being human again. He wishes a resolution to the problem he presented himself early in the novel: "He wished to return to camp, knowing that this affair was a blue demonstration; or else to go into a battle and discover that he had been a fool in his doubts, and was, in truth, a man of traditional courage." It would seem to follow that Fleming's final reflections and judgments about himself, many of which bear a pointed resemblance in phrasing to those occurring after his desertion, are no more valid than any other products of his reflection; after all, he bases his estimations on "gilded edges of memory." He may be a man of courage, but that man is certainly not the traditional one of his reflections. Crane most characteristically pursues these dilemmas, not in "The Veteran," so often read as a coda to *The Red Badge,* but in stories like "A Mystery of Heroism," in which the hero, though "sure of very little . . . had blindly been led by quaint emotions and laid himself under an obligation to walk squarely up to the face of death." Crane, too, like his character, is sure of very little, but he unflinchingly examines the enigma of a hero who is also a fool.

To say that Henry accurately summarizes and interprets his experience would deny a major premise of the novel, the gap between the mind's battleful ways and its "usual machines of reflection." Fleming's memories are naturally gilded, because what a soldier can truly recall is at most "bits of color that in the flurry had stamped themselves unawares upon his engaged senses." But for Crane to treat Henry with total irony would deny what the novel so clearly demonstrates: he does become a veteran of sorts, his public deeds are worthy of honor, and during the course of events, his eyes do open to some new ways. What Crane actually intended in his closing remarks is unknowable, but as Merleau-Ponty said somewhat facetiously, "The sum of the accidents of a novel appears as the author's intention." Several of the deletions from the manuscript version indicate that a possible intention was to reduce the irony of the final chapter, but the irony is not totally eliminated. Henry's mind was surely "undergoing a subtle change." He could criticize his acts, but only with "some correctness," and he had defeated "certain" sympathies. During his adventures there was a moment when "New eyes were given to him. And the most startling thing was to learn suddenly that he was very insignificant." However, the proud and bombastic assertions of the last chapter show that Henry considers himself at that moment as anything but insignificant. Though he does seem to show some moral maturity when he realizes he deserted the tattered soldier, Fleming, unlike Wilson or the cheery soldier, nowhere demonstrates that generosity toward others which apparently comes to one who can "perceive himself as a very wee thing." Henry looks back on a romantic figure of himself (a figure that in some ways he had actually become). The final comment on Henry's view of himself is the image of the sun breaking through a cloud. This image is not inherently positive, for in the last chapter of *Maggie* the "inevitable sunlight came streaming in at the windows" to mock Mrs. Johnson. Just as the ray of sunlight appears amid leaden rain clouds, Henry's smile and visions of tranquil skies appear amid a "procession of weary soldiers . . . despondent and muttering, marching with churning effort in a trough of liquid brown mud." Despite Henry's thirst for a soft and eternal peace, the procession, as one soldier suggests, may be "goin' down here aways, swing aroun', an' come in behint 'em." At best the ending is ambivalent. Crane does not deny that Fleming has changed (or that he momentarily feels as he does), but Crane refuses to confirm that the assessment of that change is accurate or permanent.

—Frank Bergon, *Stephen Crane's Artistry* (New York: Columbia University Press, 1975), pp. 81–82

[James Nagel (b. 1940) is the author of *Vision and Value: A Thematic Introduction to the Short Story* (1970) and the compiler of a bibliography of criticism on Sarah Orne Jewett (1978) and several critical anthologies. He is a professor of English at Northeastern University. In this extract from his book on Crane, Nagel maintains that the secret of Crane's impressionistic style in *The Red Badge of Courage* is that the third-person narrative sees all events through the eyes of Henry Fleming, who has a limited perspective on what is going on around him.]

The point of view Crane employed in *The Red Badge* is basically that of a limited third-person narrator whose access to data is restricted to the mind of the protagonist, Henry Fleming, to his sensory apprehensions and associated thoughts and feelings. In typical Impressionistic manner, Henry's experiences are discontinuous and fragmented and result in a novel composed of brief units. These scenes do not always relate directly to juxtaposed episodes, nor do they always develop the same themes. Furthermore, Henry's view of the battle is severely limited. He knows nothing of the strategy of the battle; he frequently cannot interpret the events around him because his information is obscured by darkness, smoke, or the noise of cannons; rumors spread quickly throughout his regiment, heightening the fear and anxiety of the men. Often, preoccupied by introspection, Henry's mind distorts the data it receives, transforming men into monsters and artillery shells into shrieking demons that leer at him. In short, Henry's view of things is limited, unreliable, and distorted, and yet a projection of the working of his mind becomes a dramatically realistic depiction of how war might appear to an ordinary private engaged in a battle in the American Civil War.

In an important sense, narrative method is the genius of *The Red Badge.* Of their own, the central events of the novel are commonplace. What gives the novel its unique quality is the method of its telling, its restriction of information. As Orm Øverland has pointed out, throughout *The Red Badge* (except in the first paragraph where, as it were, the "camera eye" settles down on the camp and the youth, and the concluding one where it again recedes) we in our imagined roles as spectators never have a larger view of the field than has the main character.

Many other Crane scholars have commented on this technique, and most of them invoke a visual metaphor, such as the "camera eye," to describe the method. Carl Van Doren, for example, wrote in the *American Mercury* in 1924 that Henry Fleming "is a lens through which a whole battle may be seen, a sensorium upon which all its details may be registered." Although Van Doren is overgenerous in his analysis of how much of the battle Henry actually sees, he is essentially correct in classifying the methodology of its rendition. Indeed, even thirty years after its initial publication, *The Red Badge* must have seemed most remarkable, for no third-person novel in American literature previously published had so severely limited its point of view. That such restriction is Impressionistic has been well established by Sergio Perosa:

> *The Red Badge of Courage* is indeed a triumph of impressionistic vision and Impressionistic technique. Only a few episodes are described from the outside; Fleming's mind is seldom analyzed in an objective, omniscient way; very few incidents are extensively *told*. Practically every scene is filtered through Fleming's point of view and seen through his eyes. Everything is related to his *vision,* to his *sense*-perception of incidents and details, to his *sense*-reactions rather than to his psychological impulses, to his confused sensations and individual impressions.

There is somewhat more "telling" by the narrator than Perosa's comment suggests, and perhaps more interplay from Henry's "psychological impulses," but this formulation of the narrative method of the novel is essentially accurate. Although there are a few passages with an intrusive narrative presence, and a few other complicating devices involving temporal dislocations, the central device of the novel is the rendering of action and thought as they occur in Henry's mind, revealing not the whole of the battle, nor even the broad significance of it, but rather the meaning of this experience to him. The immediacy of the dramatic action is a product of the rendering of the sensory data of Henry's mind; the psychological penetration results from the mingling of experience with association, distortion, fantasy, and memory. A further implication of this method, one that is unsettling but realistic, is that the world presented to Henry is beyond his control, beyond even his comprehension. His primary relation to it is not so much a matter of his deeds as of his organization of sensation into language and pattern.

—James Nagel, *Stephen Crane and Literary Impressionism* (University Park: Pennsylvania State University Press, 1980), pp. 52–53

DONALD PEASE ON THE DEATH OF JIM CONKLIN

[Donald Pease is a professor of English at Dartmouth College. He has written *Visionary Compacts: American Renaissance Writings in Cultural Contexts* (1987) and edited *National Identities and Post-Americanist Narratives* (1994). In this extract, Pease studies the effect of Jim Conklin's death on Henry Fleming, showing that it transforms his earlier fear of death into rage at the irrationality of war and thereby makes the emergence of his "courage" possible.]

In *The Red Badge of Courage,* Crane focuses less on Henry's attempts to recover coherence by imposing an interpretation than on his failures. For, as we have seen, in these failures Henry repeatedly recovers the force of his character as its inaccessibility to preexistent forms. Whereas Henry formerly elaborated this inaccessibility into compelling dreams supervised by fear, in the course of the desertion that realizes "his" dream, Henry confronts a visionary figure terrifying enough to make even his dream of fear seem ghostly by comparison. Possessed by the need to justify his desertion, Henry happens upon the figure of a dying soldier who should have provided just the occasion Henry needs to give desertion a persuasive rationale. Turned into a ghost of himself by the battle incidents that converted him into just another casualty of war and the war narrative that sacrificed his life to its purposes, this "spectral soldier" effectively marks the point of intersection of the two great forces of alienation Henry equally fears. As the horrible double effect of both battle and battle narratives, Conklin's death should have the power to provide Henry's fear with the justification even Nature failed to supply. When confronted, however, with this horrible justification, Henry does not find still another corroboration for his desertion but a limit to all attempts to justify any activity whatever. Faced with the figure swelled with the redoubled force of alienation, Henry discovers the inadequacy of every attempt at justification. When we recall that it was Conklin, waving his arms in enthusiastic sympathy with the exciting news of troop movement, who awoke Henry's earliest fears, we get a sense of the full extent of their loss. Moreover, when we perceive the spastic arm movements released by his death as after-images of the arm-waving enthusiasm that earlier accompanied Jim's tales of war, we get an uncanny sense of witnessing in this literal correlation of narration and existence not simply the destruction of Jim Conklin but the loss of the power of narration to inform existence. In this scene, Henry mourns both the loss of his friend and the loss of a narration intended to represent this loss. Upon recognizing the identity of the "spectral soldier," Henry comprehends through this terrible recognition the shadowy limitations of his great dream of fear. Conklin's death interrupts Henry's attempt to rationalize his fear at the very moment Henry needs it most urgently, or rather it permanently separates the shock enveloped within his fear from any recognition capable of relieving it. Conklin's death, as the intersection of alienating forces released by battles and narratives, thereby supplants Henry's cowardice in that charged place between actual and narrated events. Henry recovers this space, however, when he turns his urgent need to supply the rationale for his fear into rage over the absence of any rationale whatsoever. This rage expresses itself not through the constraints of discursive narratives but through the breakdown of any attempt to constrain it into meaning:

> The youth turned with sudden, livid rage toward the battlefield. He shook his fist. He seemed about to deliver a philippic.
> "Hell—"
> The red sun was pasted in the sky like a [fierce] wafer.

Instead of being discharged into a "philippic," a convention that socializes rage into a manageable expression of loss, Henry's rage breaks down into a threatening impression, one that glares back at him with all the fury of its inaccessibility to his context. In registering this impression at this moment, Crane does not secretly subscribe to the doctrine of naturalism. As a cultural movement, naturalism only justified man's advance upon nature by reflecting back the force of his encroachment as if it were the course of Nature. Nor does this impression "symbolize" Henry's reaction. Like the color that dominates it, this impression renders visible only a glaring surface. Henry's registration of this perception in place of the philippic marks a transformation in his mode of accommodating himself to events. Formerly, Henry actively ignored events and scenes his representation could not appropriate. After emptying Henry's perception of such vast ideological issues as the liberation of the slaves and the recovery of the Union, Crane investigates perception reduced, as it were, to its least common denominators. In the absence of abstract moral and political principles, fear and shame restore coherence and significance to perception even as they circumscribe its locus. Disrespectful of the seeming irrelevance of Private Fleming's apperception to the events surrounding him, fear and shame intervene and replace Fleming's sense of the sheer contingency of what actually transpires with a conventional drama, proceeding from fear and into desertion but holding out the promise of a triumphant recovery of courage.

—Donald Pease, "Fear, Rage, and the Mistrials of Representation in *The Red Badge of Courage*," *American Realism: New Essays,* ed. Eric J. Sundquist (Baltimore: Johns Hopkins University Press, 1982), pp. 168–69

CHESTER L. WOLFORD ON THE CONFLICT BETWEEN HOMERIC AND CHRISTIAN IDEALS

[Chester L. Wolford (b. 1944), a professor of humanities and social sciences at Pennsylvania State University,

Behrend College (Erie, Pennsylvania), is the author of two books on Stephen Crane, *The Anger of Stephen Crane* (1983) and *Stephen Crane: A Study of the Short Fiction* (1989). In this extract from his earlier book, Wolford believes that Henry Fleming is torn between the Homeric ideal of war as a source of glory and the Christian ideal (inculcated by his mother) of resignation and humility, a conflict that is manifested in the struggle between individualism and collectivism.]

The first chapter of *The Red Badge* presents heroic ideals in the mind of Henry Fleming, a "youth" inclined by instinct toward *areté,* but checked by "religious and secular education" so that he feels himself to be a part of something much larger than himself. Henry is introduced into the story and is immediately engaged in a debate with himself over "some new thoughts that had lately come to him." On the one hand, he sees himself in expressly Homeric terms, with "peoples secure in the shadow of his eagle-eyed prowess." In retrospect, he remembers having "burned several times to enlist. Tales of great movements shook the land. They might not be distinctly Homeric, but there seemed to be much glory in them. He had read of marches, sieges, conflicts, and he had longed to see it all. His busy mind had drawn for him large pictures extravagant in color, lurid with breathless deeds." On the other hand, his mother, the voice of Christian-group ideals, "had discouraged him." Her advice upon his enlistment is the advice of the group: "Don't go a-thinkin' you can lick the hull rebel army at the start, because yeh can't. Yer just one little feller amongst a hull lot of others, and yeh've got to keep quiet an' do what they tell yeh." Contrary to Henry's Grecian mood—he would rather have heard "about returning with his shield or on it"— his mother's relationship to Christianity is everywhere apparent. Her only remark upon hearing of Henry's enlistment is "The Lord's will be done," and when he leaves she says simply, "The Lord'll take keer of us all."

As a surrogate mother, the army too puts a damper on his heated individualism. Before leaving home, "he had felt growing within him the strength to do mighty deeds of arms," but after spending "months of monotonous life in a camp," Henry comes "to regard himself as part of a vast blue demonstration."

Throughout the first half of *The Red Badge,* the competition between the individualism of Henry's *areté* and the collectivism of *pietas* and "heroic martyrdom" swings between extremes. In his first engagement, Henry seems finally to give in to the standards of the group: "He suddenly lost concern for himself and forgot to look at a menacing fate. He became not a man but a member. He felt that something of which he was a part— a regiment, an army, a cause, or a country—was in crisis. He was welded into a common personality which was dominated by a single desire." Soon, the group becomes even more important to him than the causes: "He felt the subtle battle brotherhood more potent even than the cause for which they were fighting. It was a mysterious fraternity."

Much has been made of Henry's joining the subtle brother-hood, but few remember that when the enemy makes a second charge against the regiment, the mysterious fraternity dissolves under an individuality revived by Henry's sense of self-preservation. He turns tail and runs. Although Achilles has more grace and style, the effect is the same in either case: both Henry and Achilles desert their friends in the field. To say, as many do, that Henry should be damned for his desertion is to speak from an historically narrow perspective; from an Homeric standpoint, one cannot be so quick to judge. In fact, no moral judgments necessarily result from Henry's flight. If Henry can get away with it (he does), if no one finds out about it (no one does), and if later he can perform "great deeds" (he does), then that is all that matters. By the end of the sixth chapter, Henry's individualism, his Homeric sense, seems to have won a limited victory—victory because Henry has escaped being subsumed by the group, limited because his sense of shame dogs him throughout the novel.

In the novel's first half the battle for Henry's allegiance to Homeric or Christian-group values occurs in Henry's mind. In the first six chapters, Henry's conflicting feelings need little prodding; in the second six, the action of the novel intensifies, as do attacks on his individualism. In this quarter of the novel, Henry enters the "forest chapel," sees Jim Conklin die in a Christ-like way, and is mentally and verbally assaulted by the "tattered man." Here, too, he receives his "red badge of courage."

It should not be surprising in light of the epic structure that this section of *The Red Badge* is filled with religious imagery. Much critical ink has been spilt in a controversy over whether or not Crane, given his naturalistic bent and nihilist vision, intends Jim Conklin, for example, to represent Christ, or the tattered man to represent the Christian-group ideal; many feel that Crane himself was confused about it and that the novel fails because he fails to resolve the problem. From the standpoint of examining the traditional epic qualities of the book, there is no problem. These chapters mark what ultimately becomes a failure of the Christian-group value system—with two thousand years of indoctrination behind it—to make Henry Fleming return to the fold. It is not Crane's intent to have the reader see things in a religious way, but to see Henry succumb to the pathetic fallacy of Christian-colored glasses.

> —Chester L. Wolford, *The Anger of Stephen Crane: Fiction and the Epic Tradition* (Lincoln: University of Nebraska Press, 1983), pp. 40–42

AMY KAPLAN ON CRANE'S NOVEL IN THE CONTEXT OF NEWSPAPER COVERAGE OF WARS

[Amy Kaplan is a professor of English at Mount Holyoke College. She has written *The Social Construction of American Realism* (1988) and coedited *Cultures of United States Imperialism* (1993). In this extract, Kaplan studies *The Red Badge of Courage* in the context of the newspaper coverage of wars in the 1890s, especially in the sensationalized newspapers operated by William Randolph Hearst.]

In America in the 1890s, the so-called yellow press of Hearst and Pulitzer was notorious not only for sensationalistic coverage of the Cuban rebellion and the subsequent Spanish-American War, but also for staging many of the spectacles they reported. When in 1896 the illustrator Fredric Remington complained to Hearst from Havana that nothing was happening,

Hearst reportedly responded, "You furnish the pictures and I'll furnish the war." To keep his promise, Hearst filled his front page with pictures of Spanish atrocities at the same time that he started the modern sports page. Both Hearst and Pulitzer made the news they reported by sending reporters on special spy missions, by leading rescue campaigns of Cuban ladies, or by using their own yachts—carrying their reporters—to capture Spanish refugees.

These spectacles often featured the reporter himself as their chief actor. During the international wars between the Civil War and World War I, the foreign correspondent came into being as a professional writer with a public persona. Bylines changed from "from our own correspondent" to the attribution of personal names, and headlines sometimes included the name of the reporter, as in the case of a celebrity like Crane: "STEPHEN CRANE AT THE FRONT FOR THE WORLD," "STEPHEN CRANE'S VIVID STORY OF THE BATTLE OF SAN JUAN," and "STEPHEN CRANE SKETCHES THE COMMON SOLDIER." Reporters often made themselves or their colleagues the heroes of their stories and the act of reporting the main plot. This focus turned writing into a strenuous activity and the reporter into a virile figure who rivaled the soldiers. If the private, Henry Fleming, tries to become a spectator of the same battle he fights, reporters, the professional spectators, often tried to become actors by engaging in combat. Crane himself both played and parodied the figure of the heroic correspondent by flaunting his indifference to bullets under fire and by capturing a Puerto Rican town in a mock invasion. The theatrical style of *The Red Badge of Courage* anticipates the aggrandizement of the act of reporting to overshadow the action on the battlefield.

By dramatizing the exploits of the reporter, newspapers transformed political and military conflicts in foreign colonies into romantic adventures in exotic landscapes. In addition, Crane suggests in his novel *Active Service*—based on his experience in the Greco-Turkish War—that the reporter also provided an important spectatorial function for the soldiers on the field, who

> when they go away to the fighting ground, out of the sight, out of the hearing of the world known to them and are eager to

perform feats of war in this new place they feel an absolute longing for a spectator. . . . The war correspondent arises, then, to become a sort of cheap telescope for the people at home; further still, there have been fights where the eyes of a solitary man were the eyes of the world; one spectator whose business it was to transfer, according to his ability, his visual impressions to other minds.

⟨. . .⟩ In *The Red Badge of Courage,* Crane had already developed the mechanisms of this cheap telescope by rendering the enemy invisible on the battlefield of the Civil War and by making the soldier's identity more contingent on an audience than on conflict with the foe. Many of Crane's newspaper reports call attention to the spectacular nature of the battles through techniques similar to those we have seen in his novel. In Crane's story of the Rough Riders' "gallant blunder," for example, their noise and bravado appear to be directed more toward making an impression on a domestic audience than toward using effective strategy against the enemy, and in his vivid report of the regulars charging up San Juan Hill, Crane offers the readers cues for cheering, as though he were describing a football game.

—Amy Kaplan, "The Spectacle of War in Crane's Revision of History," *New Essays on* The Red Badge of Courage, ed. Lee Clark Mitchell (Cambridge: Cambridge University Press, 1986), pp. 102–4

DONALD B. GIBSON ON WILSON

[Donald B. Gibson (b. 1933) has written *The Fiction of Stephen Crane* (1968), *The Politics of Literary Expression: A Study of Major Black Writers* (1981), and other volumes. He is a professor of English at Rutgers University. In this extract from his book on *The Red Badge of Courage,* Gibson examines the figure of Wilson, showing how he develops a mutually dependent relationship with Henry Fleming.]

His relation to Wilson may be regarded in a number of ways, as good or bad, as positive or negative. It is good in that it brings Henry out of himself and into relation with another human, which forces Henry to see things in a more objective way. Wilson acts as a check on reality and as a model of conduct. One of the reasons that Henry is able to go unflinchingly into the fourth engagement is that Wilson is with him and they are mutually supportive. They are both aware, as pointed out above, that their chances of getting back, insofar as they know, are slim. They look to each other for support and they find it in each other's faces: "The youth, turning, shot a quick inquiring glance at his friend, the latter returned to him the same manner of look." They are the only ones who know of the likelihood that they will not get back. Their decision to go forward, to participate despite their knowledge, is clearly a mutual and not individual decision. They respond as they do because they are two and not one: "They saw no hesitation in each other's faces . . ." What is to be noted is the sharp contrast between Henry's situation here and at the beginning of the novel where he is so entirely alone: "The youth, considering himself as separated from the others, was saddened by the blithe and merry speeches that went from rank to rank." "The youth kept from intercourse with his companions as much as circumstances would allow him." Initially he can hardly communicate with anyone about the most basic matters regarding what will happen to him in battle. These two look to each other for confirmation, support, and encouragement, and they find it.

At the root of the relation between Henry and Wilson is Henry's fear of being laughed at. Easily stung by disapproval, especially sharp or widespread disapproval, Henry feels that Wilson is so greatly accepting that Henry need not fear that he will judge him. Henry sees himself in the soldier who attempts to steal a horse from a farmyard. The reactions of the regiment to the struggle between the pilferer and a farm girl are typical in that the soldiers seem to thrive on belittling, berating, or otherwise discrediting each other. "They jeered the piratical private, and called attention to various defects in his personal appearance." Henry chooses to relate the incident because its effect on him is such as to remind him of the precarious situation he and his comrades are in. The slightest misstep may bring down upon one the disapprobation of everyone around. "There were crows and catcalls showered upon him when he retreated without the horse. The regiment rejoiced at his downfall." His comrades are ever on the ready to judge: more experienced soldiers call less experienced ones "fresh fish," officers refer to enlisted men as "mule drivers," or "mud slingers," the lieutenant calls Henry "lunkhead." But he knows Wilson will not judge him, and for that reason he is admitted into the inner circle of Henry's trust, but no one else is.

—Donald B. Gibson, The Red Badge of Courage: *Redefining the Hero* (Boston: Twayne, 1988), pp. 61–62, 65

DAVID HALLIBURTON ON ASTONISHMENT IN *THE RED BADGE OF COURAGE*

[David Halliburton (b. 1933), a professor of English at Stanford University, is the author of *Edgar Allan Poe: A Phenomenological View* (1973), *Poetic Thinking: An Approach to Heidegger* (1981), and a study of Stephen Crane from which this extract is taken. Here, Halliburton believes that the brevity of the chapters and scenes in *The Red Badge of Courage* is meant to heighten the sense of astonishment felt by all the characters in the novel.]

The relative brevity of Crane's chapters, sentences, and scenes is a corollary of his emphasis on the flash of astonishment, itself an aspect of his stress on sudden contrasts and shifts. His *unit of composition,* in other words, may be said to contribute as much to his impressionism and his expressionism as his use of colors or physical details. The small unit registers an immediate sharp imprint in a way that longer units (such as the sentences in Faulkner) do not. The moment of astonishment, by deepening this imprint, produces tableaux of wonder, of which the scene of the little man alone on the heights of the mesmeric mountain is an eminent example. In *The Red Badge of Courage* a tableau of this type occurs just after Henry flees the tattered man, another when he begins to get an overview of the war: "As he gazed around him, the youth felt a flash of astonishment at the blue, pure sky and the sun-gleamings on the trees and fields. It was surprising that nature had gone tranquilly on with her golden processes in the midst of so much devilment." The tableau, with a subtle force, records a particular brief state to be carried over into the next unit, where our sense of that state will be strengthened or qualified.

Crane weaves these moments of astonishment into a complex rhythm. The youth first feels amazed, then the tattered man, "filled with wonder at the tall soldier," looks on "in gaping amazement"; Henry, imagining the amazement another might feel, later feels amazement himself; amazement is then felt by a friend, but instead of rotating back to Henry it passes on to another man, then to a group: "During this moment of leisure they seemed all to be engaged in staring with astonishment at him."

Astonishment can become an all-absorbing, almost hypnotic state: "Awakening from his trance of observation, he turned and beheld the loud soldier." It is not memories that freeze you in this immobile dream-like state, it is the waking world of events, which take possession of you in two basic ways. If you identify with them, you get swept up—not until the events are over do you come to know your role in them. But if you do not identify with others—if the astonishing things always happen to someone else—you become a prisoner of your own detachment.

Within the preceding passage, the trance and the moment of awakening are brought into a single sentence, while later they are stretched out between the end of one chapter and the beginning of another. Thus, at the end of Chapter 5 Fleming feels his flash of astonishment at the blue, pure sky, but does not wake up until the beginning of the next chapter: "The youth awakened slowly. . . . So it was all over at last. The supreme trial had passed." Henry does not "wake," in other words, to a new awareness, but merely enters another phase of illusion.

Much later Henry is astonished, for example, at the illusory ideas in his own mind and later still he believes the regiment's efforts will "spread consternation and amazement for miles." Astonishment is also a quality "out there" in the world: There is amazement in the regiment as a whole, in the speed with which the sound of artillery spreads or the men get dirty, in the feelings of an enemy prisoner toward his own wound. The "sharing" of astonishment and amazement, then, is one of the paths Henry follows on his journey from isolation to fraternity. In the same connection, he wakes up to those around him; then, although in the battle heroics of Chapter 17 he forgets himself without remembering his comrades, he later feels a solidarity with the rest of his regiment. This process, frequently interrupted as it is, may be described as an irregular rhythm in which awareness advances, then recedes. It is not merely that the youth must become aware; he must become aware again and again, for between the moments of awareness come periods of oblivion: "By this struggle, he had over-come obstacles which he had admitted to be mountains. . . . And he had not been aware of the process. He had slept and, awakening, found himself a knight." Although the awakening ends this particular battle trance, in a sense it begins another one, for, Henry's comfort in the gaze of the others is too full of prideful ease; it is less difficult to wake up than to stay awake—to meet an astonishing world with unclouded eyes—and that is one of the reasons why the astonishment-driving process of coming to awareness occurs so often in the book.

—David Halliburton, *The Color of the Sky: A Study of Stephen Crane* (Cambridge: Cambridge University Press, 1989), pp. 127–29

PATRICK K. DOOLEY ON THE TATTERED MAN

[Patrick K. Dooley is a professor of philosophy at St. Bonaventure University. He has written *Pragmatism as Humanism: The Philosophy of William James* (1974) and has compiled a bibliography of criticism on Stephen Crane (1992). In this extract from his book on Crane's philosophy, Dooley studies the incident of the

tattered man—a wounded soldier whom Henry
Fleming refuses to assist—and shows that this incident
is critical in Fleming's moral development.]

Having reached the limit of his desertion, Fleming rebounds
and "began to run in the direction of the battle," where he
finds himself among the wounded, "a blood-stained crowd
streaming to the rear." Joining the retreat, he walks beside the
tattered man. Feeling like "an invader" and intolerably threat-
ened by his gentle, pleading, and responsive companion,
Fleming bolts when asked a second time, " 'Where yeh hit?' " A
short flight brings him to the spectral soldier, his friend Jim
Conklin. Later, when Fleming is rejoined by the tattered man,
both try to help Conklin. As they watch his death dance, however, they are sent away, " 'Leave me be—don't tech me—
leave me be—' "

The tattered man and Fleming continue down the road. The
tattered man, wounded in both head and arm, is more concerned about Fleming, " 'Ye'd better take keer of yer hurt. It
don't do t'let sech things go. It might be inside mostly, an'
them plays thunder. Where is it located?' " Finally, when he
asks a fourth time, " 'where is your'n located?' " Henry bristles,
" 'Oh, don't bother me. . . . Goodbye.' " As Fleming pulls away,
the tattered man, now tottering and beginning to slur his
words, accosts Fleming, " 'It ain't—right—it ain't—fer yeh
t'go—trompin' off . . . ain't right.' " As Fleming climbs a fence
and looks back, he sees the tattered man whom he has abandoned "wandering about helplessly in the fields."

In the next chapter Fleming rationalizes. His self-defense is
not about abandoning a man precisely when his efforts might
have made a significant difference. Instead, he worries about
the public specter of the desertion of his battle post. The more
wounded men he sees, the more his envy of a badge of
courage and "the black weight of his woe returned to him."
Shortly thereafter, he is accidentally "wounded" so that he can
return to his regiment with "his self-pride . . . now entirely
restored." Later, his new self-esteem is, in part, warranted by
his fierce fighting in the first wave of his regiment's attack and
then by the "sublime recklessness" of his charge as a flag
bearer. He decides that his heroism on the second day of battle

redeems his cowardice. "Later, he began to study his deeds, his failures, and his achievements. . . . At last they marched before him clearly. From this present view point he was enabled to look upon them in spectator fashion and to criticise them with some correctness . . . he felt gleeful and unregretting, for in it his public deeds were paraded in great and shining prominence. . . . He saw that he was good."

Crane then skillfully draws a distinction. Fleming's heroism during the second day of battle easily atones for his cowardice, "the ghost of his flight from the first engagement appeared to him and danced." These second-thought threats to his "pompous and veteranlike" composure were merely faint and venial irritations, "small shoutings in his brain . . . for a moment, he blushed." Quite another matter, the panic of his moral failure, ever bright and mortal, remains unredeemed. "A spectre of reproach came to him. There loomed the dogging memory of the tattered soldier—he who, gored by bullets and faint for blood, had fretted concerning an imagined wound in another; he who had loaned his last of strength and intellect for the tall soldier; he who, blind with weariness and pain, had been deserted in the field."

Fleming's guilt persists, "whichever way his thoughts turned they were followed by the somber phantom of the desertion in the fields." He finally convinces himself that his inner wound of moral failure is not evident to his companions. He becomes a man when he confronts "his vivid error . . . [and he] gradually mustered force to put the sin at a distance . . . he could look back upon the brass and bombast of his earlier gospels . . . he discovered that he now despised them."

His growth to adulthood is not due to battlefield heroics and public deeds. Rather, his quiet manhood is the fruit of three separate moral realizations: his confrontation with a serious ethical choice, his acknowledgment that he had failed to respond morally, and his most difficult and humbling experience, the decision to forgive and accept himself.
—Patrick K. Dooley, *The Pluralistic Philosophy of Stephen Crane* (Urbana: University of Illinois Press, 1993), pp. 88–89

Books by
Stephen Crane

Maggie: A Girl of the Streets (A Story of New York). 1893.

The Black Riders and Other Lines. 1895.

The Red Badge of Courage: An Episode of the American Civil War. 1895.

George's Mother. 1896.

The Little Regiment and Other Episodes of the American Civil War. 1896.

The Third Violet. 1897.

The Open Boat and Other Tales of Adventure. 1898.

War Is Kind. 1899.

Active Service. 1899.

The Monster and Other Stories. 1899.

Whilomville Stories. 1900.

Wounds in the Rain: War Stories. 1900.

Great Battles of the World. 1901.

Last Words. 1902.

The O'Ruddy: A Romance (with Robert Barr). 1903.

Men, Women and Boats. Ed. Vincent Starrett. 1921.

The Work of Stephen Crane. Ed. Wilson Follett. 1925–26. 12 vols.

Two Letters to Joseph Conrad. 1926.

Collected Poems. Ed. Wilson Follett. 1930.

A Battle in Greece. 1936.

The Sullivan Country Sketches. Ed. Melvin Schoberlin. 1949.

Love Letters to Nellie Crouse. Ed. Edwin H. Cady and Lester G. Wells. 1954.

Letters. Ed. R. W. Stallman and Lillian Gilkes. 1960.

Uncollected Writings. Ed. Olov W. Fryckstedt. 1963.

Complete Short Stories and Sketches. Ed. Thomas A. Gullason. 1963.

War Dispatches. Ed. R. W. Stallman and E. R. Hagemann. 1964.

The New York City Sketches and Related Pieces. Ed. R. W. Stallman and E. R. Hagemann. 1966.

Poems. Ed. Joseph Katz. 1966, 1972 (as *Complete Poems*).

Complete Novels. Ed. Thomas A. Gullason. 1967.

Notebook. Ed. Donald J. Greiner and Ellen B. Greiner. 1969.

The Portable Stephen Crane. Ed. Joseph Katz. 1969.

Works. Ed. Fredson Bowers. 1969–76. 10 vols.

Prose and Poetry. Ed. J. C. Levenson. 1984.

Correspondence. Ed. Stanley Wertheim and Paul Sorrentino. 1988.

Books about Stephen Crane and *The Red Badge of Courage*

Bassan, Maurice, ed. *Stephen Crane: A Collection of Critical Essays.* Englewood Cliffs, NJ: Prentice-Hall, 1967.

Beaver, Harold. "Stephen Crane: The Hero as Victim." *Yearbook of English Studies* 12 (1982): 186–92.

Beer, Thomas. *Stephen Crane: A Study in American Letters.* New York: Knopf, 1923.

Beidler, Philip D. "Stephen Crane's *The Red Badge of Courage:* Henry Fleming's Courage in Its Contexts." *CLIO* 20 (1991): 235–51.

Benfey, Christopher. *The Double Life of Stephen Crane.* New York: Knopf, 1992.

Berryman, John. *Stephen Crane.* New York: Sloane, 1950.

Binder, Henry. "*The Red Badge of Courage* Nobody Knows." *Modern Fiction Studies* 10 (1978): 9–47.

Bloom, Harold, ed. *Stephen Crane.* New York: Chelsea House, 1987.

———, ed. *Stephen Crane's* The Red Badge of Courage. New York: Chelsea House, 1987.

Breslin, Paul. "Courage and Convention: *The Red Badge of Courage.*" *Yale Review* 66 (1976–77): 209–22.

Colvert, James. *Stephen Crane.* San Diego: Harcourt Brace Jovanovich, 1984.

Conder, John. "*The Red Badge of Courage:* Form and Function." In *Modern American Fiction: Form and Function,* ed. Thomas Daniel Young. Baton Rouge: Louisiana State University Press, 1989, pp. 28–38.

Curran, John E., Jr. " 'Nobody Seems to Know Where We Go': Uncertainty, History, and Irony in *The Red Badge of Courage.*" *American Literary Realism* 26, No. 1 (Fall 1993): 1–12.

Dunn, N. E. "The Common Man's *Iliad.*" *Comparative Literature Studies* 21 (1984): 270–81.

Franchere, Ruth. *Stephen Crane.* New York: Crowell, 1961.

French, Warren. "Stephen Crane: Moment of Myth." *Prairie Schooner* 55 (1981): 155–67.

Fried, Michael. *Realism, Writing, Disfiguration: On Thomas Eakins and Stephen Crane.* Chicago: University of Chicago Press, 1987.

Frohock, W. M. "*The Red Badge of Courage* and the Limits of Parody." *Southern Review* 6 (1970): 137–48.

Gibson, Donald B. *The Fiction of Stephen Crane.* Carbondale: Southern Illinois University Press, 1968.

Gilkes, Lillian Barnard. *Cora Crane: A Biography of Mrs. Stephen Crane.* Bloomington: Indiana University Press, 1960.

Greenfield, Stanley B. "The Unmistakable Stephen Crane." *PMLA* 73 (1958): 562–72.

Gullason, Thomas A., ed. *Stephen Crane's Career: Perspectives and Evaluations.* New York: New York University Press, 1972.

Hoffman, Daniel G. *The Poetry of Stephen Crane.* New York: Columbia University Press, 1957.

Holton, Milne. *Cylinder of Vision: The Fiction and Journalistic Writing of Stephen Crane.* Baton Rouge: Louisiana State University Press, 1972.

Karlen, Arno. "The Craft of Stephen Crane." *Georgia Review* 28 (1974): 470–84.

Katz, Joseph, ed. *Stephen Crane in Transition: Centenary Essays.* DeKalb: Northern Illinois University Press, 1972.

Knapp, Bettina L. *Stephen Crane.* New York: Ungar, 1987.

LaFrance, Marston. *A Reading of Stephen Crane.* Oxford: Clarendon Press, 1971.

Lavers, Norman. "Order in *The Red Badge of Courage.*" *University of Kansas City Review* 32 (1966): 287–95.

Lee, A. Robert. "Stephen Crane's *The Red Badge of Courage:* The Novella as 'Moving Box.'" In *The Modern American Novella,* ed. A. Robert Lee. New York: St. Martin's Press, 1989, pp. 30–47.

Linson, Corwin K. *My Stephen Crane.* Syracuse, NY: Syracuse University Press, 1971.

Mariani, Giorgio. *Spectacular Narratives: Representations of Class and War in Stephen Crane and the American 1890s.* New York: Peter Lang, 1992.

Modern Fiction Studies 5, No. 3 (Fall 1959). Special Stephen Crane issue.

Mulcaire, Terry. "Progressive Visions of War in *The Red Badge of Courage* and *The Principles of Scientific Management.*" *American Quarterly* 43 (1991): 46–72.

Nichols, Prescott S. "*The Red Badge of Courage:* What Is Fleming Fleeing?" *Literature & History* 12 (1986): 97–102.

Parker, Hershel. *Flawed Texts and Verbal Icons: Literary Authority in American Fiction.* Evanston, IL: Northwestern University Press, 1984.

Pizer, Donald. "*The Red Badge of Courage:* Text, Theme, and Form." *South Atlantic Quarterly* 84 (1985): 302–13.

Rogers, Rodney. "Stephen Crane and Impressionism." *Nineteenth-Century Fiction* 24 (1969): 292–304.

Schneider, Michael. "Monomyth Structure in *The Red Badge of Courage.*" *American Literary Realism* 20, No. 1 (Fall 1987): 45–55.

Schneider, Robert W. "Stephen Crane: The Promethean Revolt." In Schneider's *Five Novelists of the Progressive Era.* New York: Columbia University Press, 1965, pp. 60–111.

Seltzer, Mark. "The Love-Master." In *Engendering Men: The Question of Male Feminist Criticism,* ed. Joseph A. Boone and Michael Cadden. New York: Routledge, 1990, pp. 140–58.

Shaw, Mary Neff. "Henry Fleming's Heroics in *The Red Badge of Courage:* A Satiric Search for a 'Kindler, Gentler' Heroism." *Studies in the Novel* 22 (1990): 418–28.

Shulman, Robert. "Community, Perception, and the Development of Stephen Crane: From *The Red Badge of Courage* to 'The Open Boat.'" *American Literature* 50 (1978): 441–60.

Solomon, Eric. *Stephen Crane: From Parody to Realism.* Cambridge, MA: Harvard University Press, 1966.

———. *Stephen Crane in England: A Portrait of the Artist.* Columbus: Ohio State University Press, 1965.

Stallman, R. W. *Stephen Crane: A Biography.* New York: George Braziller, 1968.

Stephen Crane Studies. 1992– .

Studies in the Novel 10, No. 1 (Spring 1978). Special Stephen Crane issue.

Van Meter, Jan R. "Sex and War in *The Red Badge of Courage:* Cultural Themes and Literary Criticism." *Genre* 7 (1974): 71–90.

Weiss, Daniel. *"The Red Badge of Courage." Psychoanalytic Review* 52 (1952): 32–52, 130–54.

Wertheim, Stanley, and Paul M. Sorrentino. *The Crane Log: A Documentary Life of Stephen Crane 1871–1900.* New York: G. K. Hall, 1994.

Wolford, Chester L. *Stephen Crane: A Study of the Short Fiction.* Boston: Twayne, 1989.

Index of
Themes and Ideas